The Exporter's & Importer's Handbook on
Foreign Currencies

The Exporter's & Importer's Handbook on
Foreign Currencies

A. D. P. Edwards

MACMILLAN
REFERENCE
BOOKS

First published 1990 by
THE MACMILLAN PRESS LTD
London and Basingstoke

Associated companies in Auckland, Delhi, Dublin,
Gaborone, Hamburg, Harare, Hong Kong, Johannesburg,
Kuala Lumpur, Lagos, Manzini, Melbourne, Mexico City,
Nairobi, New York, Singapore, Tokyo.

British Library Cataloguing in Publication Data

Edwards, Derrick
    The exporters and importers handbook on foreign
    currencies.
    1. Foreign exchange
    I. Title
    332.45

    ISBN 0-333-53419-0

Typeset and printed in Great Britain

To those exporters and importers who have over many years given me so generously of their friendship and encouragement, I dedicate this book.

Contents

Contents

Introduction

This book is based on nearly forty years experience of working closely with all manner of industrial and commercial companies in the fields of export credits, export finance and foreign exchange. It has been written in layman's terms avoiding jargon and is designed to show how the foreign exchange market works and how exporters and importers can and should be using its facilities so as to obtain, without incurring exchange risks, the benefits which its proper uses can bestow. These have a direct bearing on a company's overseas marketing, pricing and purchasing strategy and it is hoped that the book will assist all those concerned in the formation of that strategy and especially those executives involved with the negotiation of overseas sales and the purchase of overseas supplies.

It is an extraordinary paradox that on the one hand the City of London has developed over the years a range of facilities far in excess of that which any other country can provide, thereby giving to British manufacturers substantial advantages over their foreign competitors, while on the other we make little use of those facilities because we do not understand them and consequently are afraid of them even at the highest management levels.

While the payment of our imports in foreign currency is widespread and appears not to cause any anxiety, seemingly because of a blissful ignorance, the sale of our goods overseas in foreign currency on the other hand still seems to conjure up all kinds of fears. 'But we are engineers not bankers, we don't play the money market', is the cry that invariably goes up when talking to executives about the need for their companies to sell overseas in foreign currencies as opposed to sterling.

Approximately 70 per cent of Britain's exports are still

invoiced in sterling. As on average we have consistently had higher interest rates in Britain than any of the other major economies over the last thirty years except for Italy and as the forward market is based on the difference in interest rates, every time we invoice an export to these countries in sterling we lose the premium arising from the lower interest rate in the foreign country and every time we pay for an import from these countries in foreign currencies we pay the premium arising from the higher interest rate at home. Alternatively, an export sale currently transacted in sterling has to be funded out of a sterling overdraft at a rate, at the time of writing, of 15 per cent per annum whereas an export sale to Germany transacted in Deutschmarks can be funded out of a Euro-Deutschmark overdraft at approximately 8 per cent per annum, all without any unjustifiable exchange risk.

An exporter of consumer goods selling to his French distributing subsidiary in sterling was making himself far less competitive in that market than was necessary. The distributor had to fix French franc prices and hold them for twelve months but carried the exchange risk. In order to protect himself therefore, he was loading his French franc prices by as much as 15 per cent. By way of a Euro French franc overdraft at a lower cost than his sterling overdraft the exporter was able to provide his distributor with fixed French franc prices for twelve months at a lower cost and without running an exchange risk.

In terms of marketing and pricing strategy, a British exporter's money may be costing him 15 per cent per annum whereas his German competitor's money may only be costing him approximately 8 per cent per annum and in those terms it is not difficult to understand why the German is beating him to the post and getting the business.

By selling in Deutschmarks the British exporter is merely plugging himself into the lower German interest rate and can thereby reduce his Deutschmark price by the whole of the differential if necessary in order to see off the competition.

This not only applies to sales to Germany but equally to sales to other countries where the British exporter is faced with German competition. Bearing in mind that if the buyer in that country decides to buy from Germany he is going to have to pay in Deutschmarks in any case, he can equally pay the British exporter in Deutschmarks.

A leading British construction company had quoted in sterling for a £3m contract in Egypt. Their agent in Egypt advised them that they were up against German competition and would have to find a 6 per cent reduction in their price in order to be in the running. This was not possible in sterling but by switching out of sterling into Deutschmarks, the premium on the forward sale of Deutschmarks over the five-year repayment period yielded an additional profit margin of no less than 15 per cent on the face value of the contract. They therefore offered a Deutschmark price less the required 6 per cent and won the contract.

If the British exporter is fully competitive in sterling, then he has already made up the differential in the interest rates and he can keep it as additional profit to that already built into the price of his product.

Without in any way underestimating the overall problems incurred by British industry over the years through the imposition of high interest rates, it is difficult to understand why those agencies set up to assist the promotion of exports have not proclaimed from the house-tops that by selling in foreign currencies the exporter can obtain the benefit of the buying country's lower interest rate and without running an exchange risk. Instead we have only had groans and complaints to the politicians that we cannot compete in export markets with such high rates.

With total annual exports in 1988 (excluding oil) of approximately £80 billion, the evidence points to the fact that by selling

overseas in sterling British exporters are allowing hundreds of
millions of pounds in additional net profit or increased competitiveness to go by default. Moreover, with regard to our imports,
we are also paying large sums by way of premiums because we
pander to the demands of our overseas suppliers to pay in their
currencies instead of insisting that we pay in sterling. The world
is in a buyer's market and any exporting executive used to
negotiating overseas sales contracts will confirm that he has to
pander to the whims of the buyer. How is it then that in Britain
our buyers seem to have to pander to the whims of the salesmen?
One buyer with overseas purchases running into many millions
of pounds a year when confronted with this situation retorted
that his overseas suppliers insisted that he pay in their currencies
otherwise they would not supply him. It is difficult to believe
that any supplier from any country, let alone one supplying
many millions of pounds worth of goods every year, is going to
throw away good export business simply because the buyer
wants to pay in his own currency. We not only live in a buyer's
market but Britain has one of the highest ratios in the world of
imports per head of population and if our buyers cannot do a
spot of insisting no one can.

When purchasing direct from an overseas supplier in sterling
and particularly when purchasing imported goods from a UK
agent in sterling, a good working knowledge of the technology is
essential in order to establish the 'correct' price as opposed to
what merely appears to be 'good' price.

*A major British company had been quoted a fixed sterling price
for a purchase from a Spanish supplier with payment in ten
months. It was a very competitive sterling price and the buyer
thought he had obtained for himself a very good deal until it was
pointed out that if the Spaniard was selling in sterling then he
had an exchange risk. In order to protect himself over the ten
months period he would load the sterling price by say 10–15 per
cent to give himself a cushion against any adverse fluctuations in
the exchange rate over the ensuing ten months. As a result the*

> *UK buyer was not getting as keen a price as he might have obtained if he paid in pesetas when the Spaniard would have no exchange risk and therefore no need to load the price. What is more, if the buyer had paid the supplier in pesetas he could have bought the pesetas forward at the time he placed the order at a discount of 8 per cent. So, while he had a good-looking sterling price he was in fact paying somewhere in the region of 18–23 per cent too much for his purchase.*

The reasons for this extraordinary but unfortunate situation are many and varied but nearly all based on ignorance and misunderstanding of a technology which has been surrounded with mystique and mumbo-jumbo for so long that executives have often been reluctant to get involved in an area which they see as being fraught with risk and speculation. For a country which has had an appalling struggle over the last fifty years in order to survive however, and which will continue to have to struggle in an increasingly competitive environment, it seems an absurdity that the majority of its international traders are still not in possession of all the factors that can impinge so severely on their profitability and competitiveness.

Blame is equally widespread. It could be argued that the banks should have done more to bring it to the notice of their clients. In defence, the banks will claim that they will always provide help and advice whenever asked. Unfortunately, it is sometimes difficult to make a request if you do not really know what to ask for. Moreover, it is the application of the technology to commercial transactions which is essential and banks rarely claim to be able to give expert advice on the shape of a commercial transaction. So far as the banks' clients are concerned, the banks are suppliers of certain services and as with all suppliers the buyer should know what he wants and what to ask for. Unfortunately, in this case very few know what to ask for and even fewer can spot a wrong answer if they get one.

'I'm up to my eyes in the end of year accounts and annual budgets. I simply don't have the time to think about additional profit.'

This *cri de cœur* came from the finance director of a manufacturing company, 40 per cent of whose output is exported. 'We sell overseas in sterling whenever possible. Like that we don't run any exchange risk. In any case our overheads are in sterling so we have to sell in sterling. Our job is to make valves not to gamble in foreign exchange. Goodbye'.

The short sharp telephone conversation came to an abrupt end. It did however, encapsulate one of the basic problems confronting British manufacturing industry in its endeavours overseas. Is top management heaping too much responsibility on to the shoulders of its accountants simply because it does not understand the true nature of the problems involved?

When the question of foreign currencies, almost entirely US dollars, began to emerge in the early 1950s, senior management assumed it was solely a question of finance and dumped the responsibility on the desk of the finance director. Although knowing very little about it, 'finance' found over the years that this newfangled magic called foreign exchange improved the status of the accountant no end and enhanced his position in the company. As a result he was understandably reluctant to relinquish that responsibility and to redirect at least part of it towards those departments more immediately involved, i.e. sales/marketing and purchasing. The result is all too often the kind of situation described above with the additional problem of 'finance', 'marketing' and 'purchasing' tending to work in isolation and sometimes with unfortunate results.

The buyer from a British company importing an expensive machine tool obtained quotations from France and Switzerland. On converting the quotations into sterling at the 'spot' rate of exchange he was pleased to discover that their prices were very competitive, so competitive in fact that there was little difference in the cost of the two products. He decided therefore to place the order with the Swiss supplier and then passed the deal to 'finance'. Finance went to buy the currency forward only to discover that whereas the French franc was at a discount against sterling of 10½ per cent the Swiss franc was at a premium of 7 per cent. While there was little difference between the cost of the two products there was 17½ per cent difference in the cost of buying the two currencies. The buyer had obviously gone to the wrong country let alone the wrong supplier.

Top management must also accept its share of the blame. While on the one hand it seems continually to be in hot pursuit of technical advances, mergers and acquisitions with all the administrative restructuring involved, on the other hand it may have lost sight of some of the simple basic issues such as the fact that the proper use of currencies in the sales and purchasing processes can in many cases provide very substantial additional profit. In fact rather more profit than the introduction of some new technologies. For example, sales to Germany, Holland, Switzerland and Japan transacted in local currencies instead of sterling in 1989 could have achieved approximate reductions in the cost of borrowing of no less than 6.48, 6.18, 6.55 and 8.14 per cent per annum respectively. These can be seen as savings in costs or increased profit/competitiveness on existing business and there are not many companies who can claim such additional margins from the introduction of new machines or new technology. Similarly, an exercise to cut the cost of production will entail much heart searching, some redundancies and an eventual cut in cost of perhaps 1 per cent.

While it is difficult for senior management to know of all new developments and fully understand them, they are eventually bound to arrive at a sufficient level of understanding in order to make an executive decision. It seems extraordinary therefore, that there should be such a lack of appreciation in the advantages which are available from the proper use of currencies and which have been readily available for the last 35 years. This lack of awareness at the top permeates the whole corporate body and is particularly noticeable in large groups. Although the corporate strategy may be one of de-centralisation with each unit its own profit centre, this lack of awareness at the top makes all the units fearful of trying anything different. 'We don't want to attract the attention of HQ by doing anything different from what we've been doing in the past', is the kind of comment heard among the subsidiaries of our conglomerates and large groups. 'If they had wanted us to sell in foreign currencies they would have told us.' As a result, hundreds of millions of pounds in export sales are transacted in sterling and large amounts of additional net profit are lost by default.

If the chairmen of such companies, responsible for their performances to shareholders, knew that the profits could have been substantially improved there is no doubt that they would have implemented a policy of selling overseas in foreign currencies. The great problem, however, is getting them to understand the technology sufficiently to be able to overcome the resistance of their senior colleagues. Comments such as 'If the Chairman knew that I require training in this field he might well ask, "What are we paying you for?"' are not unknown.

In view of the huge sums of additional profit and/or increased competitiveness involved one also has to ask why the investment managers and consultants and no less the stockbrokers themselves have not made their voices heard on this issue. After all they are considered to be the guardians of the investing public. Can it possibly be that even they do not fully appreciate the benefits which can accrue from the proper use of this technology?

In the light of all the evidence one has to conclude that there is urgent need to dispel the ignorance that still prevails in so many places and to provide appropriate training especially to those executives responsible for overseas sales and purchases. Training managers may be doing what they can to keep their companies' senior personnel aware of new developments and technologies but in most cases they merely do the bidding of senior management. If a company's board is sold on the idea that it should extend its expertise in some particular direction, the board will give instructions to the training manager accordingly. It is rare to find a training manager who is prepared to take the initiative and press for training on a subject when that subject may not be fully understood at board level.

The firms of management consultants and even some of the colleges of management training do not yet seem to have recognised the need for such training. They cover many facets of marketing and salesmanship but slide gently over the subject of foreign exchange as coming within the orbit of 'finance'. While the finance department of a company may have the responsibility for managing the currency exposure once a currency commitment has been made, it is the direct application of the technology to the actual negotiation of the sales and purchases which is essential if maximum benefit is to be achieved.

Foreign exchange has almost entirely been seen in the past as a cause of risk and consequently lectures and seminars on the subject have been based on the avoidance of risk and very little else. Very few have emphasised the positive aspect of understanding how the system works and of using the available facilities properly. Such action will not only avoid the risks but provide very substantial benefit. As with electricity, which can be extremely dangerous if not used properly, the use of foreign currencies in both exports and imports demands a disciplined approach in order to avoid risk. As with electricity however, this does not mean 'leave well alone'. If it did, we should still be in the age of candles and oil-lamps.

The book falls into two parts. Part I describes how the 'system' works starting with a background to foreign exchange and the emergence of the Euro-dollar, describing what it is and the subsequent development of the Euro-currency market. It explains the figures which are published every day on the currency page of the *Financial Times* and goes into considerable detail regarding the forward market, premiums and discounts and how they are calculated from the difference in Euro-currency interest rates. It provides brief details sufficient for the busy executive to understand the meaning and function of currency futures and currency options. It goes into some detail on the function of the European Currency Unit (ECU), its growth and its potential use as the means of stabilising prices throughout the EEC.

Part II of the book is devoted to the application of the various techniques to commercial transactions and their effect on marketing, pricing and purchasing strategy. It provides many case studies of both exports and imports showing the very substantial advantages available in the proper use of foreign currencies. It emphasises the fact that these do not arise from or entail risk or speculation. The final stages list the major strategic considerations and give some emphasis on the purchase of foreign goods in sterling through UK import agents.

The book is designed to take the reader through the various techniques stage by stage and should therefore be followed in sequence. Once the technology has been mastered, it will provide an invaluable point of reference.

Part I
The Technology
(How the System Works)

1 A Background to Foreign Exchange

'Money is like a sixth sense without which you cannot make a complete use of the other five' – *Of Human Bondage* by Somerset Maugham

For most people, the term foreign exchange conjures up a vision of a holiday spent abroad, crossing national frontiers and culminating in an accumulation of surplus assorted foreign coins and low value notes, so coveted by the child collector. In the context of the EEC, these might comprise varying denominations of national currency units, such as the franc, guilder, krone, mark, peseta and lira, interspersed with lower denominations of centime, cent, ore and pfennig thrown in for good measure. But there is much more to foreign exchange – conversion of one currency into another – in its application to international trading than in its relation to travel and tourism, despite the expansion of the latter into a global industry involving the same two-way flow of currencies.

The dawn of trade began with a system of barter, the exchange of goods for goods. The products and tools of hunting doubtless figured in the earliest exchanges – skins, furs, spears, daggers, axeheads and arrows in a ratio perhaps of one spear equals three axes equals twelve arrows. But before dismissing barter as an antiquated, outmoded form of trade engaged in by our primitive ancestors, let us not forget the modern barter deals of Eastern Europe involving the exchange of Russian watches, furs and oil for cereals or Romanian foodstuffs for machine tools consequent on the non-convertibility of Comecon currencies. Nor indeed, the sophisticated barter transaction when the Italian Fiat car manufacturer successfully contracted to build, in the USSR, a complete automobile production plant based on Fiat operational design, technology and expertise to be subsequently paid for in cars which rolled off the selfsame production line. Consider the implications of this 'barter' deal, denuded of a monetary role, safeguards or penalty clauses, in which Fiat, on the one hand, secured a substantial order in the face of keen competition, and the Russians on the other the best of all possible guarantees as to quality and timely commissioning!

The increasing diversity and inequality of the goods exchanged by way of barter led to a growing demand for a common medium of exchange and eventually to the development of money. The pre-money era saw many strange objects used for this purpose; some useful, like nails and fish-hooks, and others useless like glass beads and the ubiquitous cowrie shell found along the shores of the Indian Ocean stretching from the eastern coast of the African continent to the western coast of Australia. Certain basic commodities, such as rock salt in North African Saharan territories and bricks of compressed tea in China were also traded in barter deals. Both commodities lasted well and being capable of sub-division could be adapted to a variety of purchases.

The Museum of Athens and the British Museum have many specimens of early coins, some dating back 2600 years. Certainly, coins were struck albeit crudely by today's electronic mass-minting standards, and were used as a medium of exchange long before Christ overthrew the tables of the money changers in the temple precincts of Jerusalem. Here the silver denarius, bearing Caesar's image, rubbed shoulders with the coins of Greece, Egypt, Asia Minor, Syria and further afield and quite possibly with the vast mintage bearing the effigy of Alexander the Great which continued to be struck 150 years after his death, by which time the Greeks had elevated him to a place in the Pantheon.

Coins were initially struck in gold or silver with the metal content matching the face value, followed by copper or bronze coins for lower denominations. But as precious metals became scarce and money in short supply, emperors, monarchs and governments were not slow to spot and pursue a course of 'wealth creation' by reducing the precious metal content through clipping the edges and thereby debasing the coinage while retaining the face value of the coins. The Roman silver denarius of the early Christian era suffered this fate at the hands of Emperor Tiberius, with 'Divini Tiberie' inscribed on the coin, as the means of resolving the short funding of his widely scattered legions. Because of his imperious, extravagant life-style and expensive foreign policy, Henry VIII also found himself short of money and resorted to debasement of the Angel-noble, the gold coin worth a third of a pound struck in the reign of Edward III. This was done by striking an inferior gold coin but retaining its former value which depicted archangel Michael evicting 'the dragon' Satan on the obverse. Having lost some of its 'nobility', the new coin came to be known as the Angel.

Crœsus, King of Lydia (Asia Minor), 560–546 BC, was the first ruler to establish a coinage in gold and silver and for centuries in the Middle East and parts of Asia, gold has been the yardstick of individual wealth. There is nowhere more so than in India where, despite the abject poverty of millions, the custom of paying dowries in gold requires even the poorest to pursue its acquisition, however meagre, in the form of jewellery for bridal adornment. The total of privately held gold, in all forms, in India probably exceeds that held in any other country including France where many housewives have a small brick or two concealed amongst the groceries as a hedge against inflation. Despite the Indian Government's legislation to stem or control the inflow of gold smuggled in sailing dhows from the Persian Gulf to one of the many small west coast ports, it continued apace.

The Royal Mint's gold sovereign, originally worth one pound, was first issued by Henry VII in 1489 and continued up to the time of James I. It was revived by George III and has continued to be minted ever since. It weighs approximately 8 grammes and is made of 22-carat gold. Its free circulation in Saudi Arabia in the post-war years of the reign of King Ibn Saud, stemmed from ARAMCO's (Arabian American Co's) contractual obligation to pay all oil royalties in gold sovereigns. Monthly shipments were air-freighted to Jeddah where the government's clearing agent took delivery and transferred the sovereigns to the government's bankers, The Netherlands Trading Society. Here a number of 'tellers' brought in from the local *Sukh* would squat in a circle around the glittering pile of sovereigns on the spacious floor, and preparatory to counting, commence sorting those with Queen Victoria's head from those with King Edward VII's and George V's head in order to facilitate slight discounts for loss of weight through protracted usage. The fact that the entire operation in transferring the gold from the plane to the bank's strongroom was overtly conducted with little or no regard to security, only serves to reflect the Draconian penalties of the law relating to theft – severing of the right hand for the first offence and beheading for the second.

Perhaps the best known example of the converse of debasement is the old Saudi riyal, which was widely regarded in the early post-war years as the finest silver coin in the world. This fact soon rendered it attractive to the dual operators in hoarding and smuggling at the east coast Gulf ports, whence it followed the old gold route to India. This caused much discomfiture to the then Saudi government, which eschewed the notion of introducing paper currency because they feared the Nejdi tribesmen, passionately loyal to the ruling family, might rebel when it came to the monarch dispensing largess. The silver riyal, now a collector's coin, has long since disappeared from circulation and been superseded by a range of paper currency, which enjoys world-wide confidence and since 1986 a fixed exchange rate against the US dollar of 3.75 riyals. This arose as a consequence of oil price increases in 1974 and 1979 and the recognition of Saudi Arabia as the dominant member of OPEC, the largest single producer of crude in the world and possessor of the largest known reserves.

With the establishment of money as a medium of exchange in inter-state trade, the parity of one currency in terms of another became the stock in trade of the moneylenders, who first practised their profession in the market squares of major commercial towns of Northern Italy, seated on a 'banca', the Italian word for bench, as well as for bank. Indeed, it was the Lombards, a group of merchant moneylenders and traders from these independent cities (called the Lombard League) who left the Plain of Lombardy in the twelfth century to settle in London, initially as the financial agents of the Popes who had many dues to collect. They had their offices in the street which still bears their name and were responsible for many innovations to assist traders, one of which in particular may be of special interest to the reader. When a trader who was intending to make a purchase across a state boundary and also wished to take advantage of a favourable exchange rate some time before making the purchase, they conceived the idea of lending him the money with which to buy the currency at the favourable exchange rate and then allowing him to put the bought currency on deposit with them at a fixed rate of interest until the time when he wished to make the purchase. As a result of this arrangement the purchaser was able to fix the exchange rate for the currency long before he needed to make the purchase and the cost of the transaction was the difference between the interest he had to pay on the borrowing and the interest he was going to earn on the deposit.

Following the expulsion of the Jews from England in 1290 the Lombards began to enjoy a special sphere of influence as lenders to the Crown as well as to those in arrears with the Pope's tithes. The royal patronage started with Henry III and continued through to Edward III who borrowed so freely that the Lombard bankers began to look to their securities, but their caution came too late and two of the three major firms were bankrupted with unpaid royal debts of 900,000 and 600,000 crowns. Up-and-coming English merchants stepped into the breach with the Lombards being finally expelled from the Kingdom by Queen Elizabeth who disapproved of their usurious activities.

It was not until the 17th century that the first European Central banks were founded. Certain major commercial cities became the recognized centres of banking, notably London, Amsterdam, Paris, Brussels, Frankfurt, Zurich and Milan. The Bank of Amsterdam (1609) takes pride of place chronologically, followed by the more prestigious Bank of England (1694).

Post-First World War, Germany saw hyper-inflation rampant, its currency virtually worthless and printing presses turning out postage stamps and currency notes bearing value figures of 'million' and 'milliard'. The most telling story was that of the

German housewife who left her wicker basket crammed with the new paper currency on the laundry floor momentarily, while she went next door. On her return, she found the basket missing and the currency notes scattered on the floor!

Post-war situations invariably find the vanquished nation subjected to crushing reparations, annexation of territory, its industry in ruins, many towns and cities reduced to rubble and its currency system collapsed. In such a situation Germany found herself twice in the first half of this century, and twice the nation succeeded, over a protracted period of struggle, discipline and self-sacrifice, to rebuild its shattered industry and restore its economy. This in spite of limitations, strictures and overall control imposed by the victors through an army of occupation.

On the economic side, the major banks found themselves largely owning what was left of industry in settlement of debts. And so it transpired that the German banks emerged holding the majority equity in industry in stark contrast with Britain, where the institutions are the principal shareholders.

Exchange control regulations were introduced in 1939 in order to conserve UK gold and foreign currency and to support the role of sterling as a major trading and reserve currency. They were also designed to restrict the outflow of sterling for purposes other than bona fide trade and monitor through customs and excise, the timely payment of trading debts. When exchange controls were abolished on 23 October 1979 the effect on the foreign exchange market, investment abroad, and forward dealing in particular, was momentous and it took both exporters and importers some time to appreciate their new-found freedom. No longer was it obligatory for the proceeds of export sales to be repatriated within six months from date of shipment! Indeed, the dismantling of exchange controls meant greater freedom to companies and individuals for investment and movement of funds around the world. With North Sea oil revenues continuing to grow and an apparently healthy balance-of-trade surplus, the government's funding of the economy, despite the outflow of capital seemed set fair. But that was before the subsequent sharp fall in the price of oil, rising value of imports, balance-of-trade deficits and weakening of sterling began to emerge. The consequent need to redress these adverse effects engendering inflationary pressures led once again to rising interest rates. Once again, however, British industry was not fully geared to take advantage of the techniques whereby they could mitigate the damage by making greater use of the Euro-currency market.

2 The Euro-currency Market

There is a great deal of confusion in people's minds about a Euro-dollar. Most think that it is a different kind of dollar. In actual fact a Euro-dollar is an ordinary US dollar but it is owned by someone who is domiciled outside the USA. Indeed, at the beginning of the Euro-currency market they were all Euro-dollars. Today it covers all the main currencies; Euro-sterling; Euro-deutschmark; Euro-yen; Euro-dollars etc. and all that is meant by Euro-currencies are currencies which are owned by people, mainly bankers, who are domiciled outside the countries of origin.

The Euro-currency market all began after the Second World War when by way of Marshall aid the Americans poured billions of dollars into Europe to help reconstruct the economies of Europe. These dollars were not loans, they were grants and Churchill put it as the most generous act by any one nation to any other nation in the history of man. As those countries began to piece themselves together, sweep away the debris, build new factories, those factories began to make goods, make profits, generate wealth. Gradually over the years, therefore, those dollars became surplus to their requirements but as they were grants and not loans which had to be repaid no one quite knew at the time how best they should be managed. The City therefore decided to establish a market for them in London and that market became known as the Euro-dollar market, i.e. surplus dollars out of Europe. As other countries began to generate a surplus of their own currencies, these also found their way into the London market and the Euro part stuck.

In establishing this market however, London was up against a problem in so far that no country much likes foreign banks coming in because they will obviously take a certain amount of

20

business away from the domestic banks. Nevertheless London took the view that if it was going to have a market-place the only one worth having was a big one, so instead of trying to keep foreign banks out it decided to try and entice as many of the world's banks into the market-place and create as big a market as possible.

The first ones in, needless to say, were the American banks. In the late 1940s/early 1950s many of them began to open branches in the City of London with the object of attracting those Euro-dollars as deposits. By June 1967 the sterling value of all Euro-dollars which had been placed on deposit almost entirely with American banks in London, was £3154m of which no less than £3067m, i.e. 97 per cent were all fed back to the USA.

By June 1987 the number of foreign banks represented on the London money market had swollen to approximately 500 together with approximately 100 British banks making a total of approximately 600 banks. This constitutes by far the largest money market in the world. Similarly, the volume of Euro-currencies deposited in London with all those banks had swollen to a value of approximately £472 billion out of which approximately £456 billion was fed back overseas.

These huge sums can be seen as the world's surplus liquidity and the Euro-currency market can be summarised as the world's banks dealing in the world's surplus liquidity. Over the years, however, it has been allowed to develop into a 'free' market and in their dealings on the Euro-currency market banks are establishing 'market interest rates' for all the major currencies. These are distinct from the internal interest rates which are imposed on those currencies at home by the politicians of the countries concerned. For example, in August 1989 while the US prime rate, which governs domestic interest rates in the USA, was 11 per cent per annum, the 3 months Euro-dollar was being traded at $8\frac{3}{4}$ per cent per annum.

While Euro-currency interest rates are governed by market forces, i.e. the law of supply and demand, they are nevertheless interrelated with their domestic interest rates. Moreover, the politicians keep a watchful eye on the free market rates as a guide to their economic policies.

The Euro-currency market has therefore become of paramount importance and especially because it is the main market in which all the world's banks are dealing when transacting their international business.

3   Premiums and Discounts

Every time anyone sells or buys any product or service across any national frontier on terms other than immediate cash payment, there is a differential in the value of the two currencies and that differential does not go away. It can either be a plus quantity or it can be a minus quantity. For example, a UK exporter selling into say Holland invoicing his buyer in guilders and expecting to receive 50,000 guilders in three months time, could ring up any bank and sell them to the bank at a premium for conversion into sterling at a future date.

The exporter can now earn extra profit from the sale to the bank of his guilders. This is over and above the profit which he is going to make from the sale of his product. What exporter in his right mind can afford not to know what that additional profit is? In any event it does not go away. He can either make himself more profit or of course he can reduce his guilder price to the buyer and thereby make himself more competitive if necessary.

Conversely, if an exporter selling to Italy in 1987 was expecting to receive say 10m Italian lire in three months time and rang up a bank in order to sell those lire to the bank for delivery and conversion at a future date, the bank would buy them off him at a discount, which meant that every time he sold lire to the bank for future delivery he was going to lose money. Some people might therefore be tempted to assume that if you are going to lose money every time you sell lire to the bank for future delivery the obvious thing is not to invoice in lire, but they would be mistaken. The reason for this is explained in Chapter 15, 'Marketing and Sales'.

You will see in Table 1 a schedule of the thirteen main trading currencies over the nineteen years 1971–1989 and the three months Average Premiums and Discounts. This schedule constitutes 242

Table 1   Premium Discount. Average 3 months premium/discount against sterling on 'forward' sale of undermentioned currencies. Percentages per annum. ( ) = Discount.

Year	US dollar	Canadian dollar	Dutch guilder	Belgian franc	Danish krone	Deutsch-mark	Italian lira	Norwegian krone	French franc	Swedish krona	Austrian schilling	Swiss franc	Japanese yen	Average London Bank Rate
1971	0.75	1.09	2.08	2.04	(1.73)	1.86	1.50	1.80	2.55	0.31	2.13	4.05		5.92 Base rate
1972	1.83	1.24	4.68	2.97	(1.18)	4.29	0.26	1.25	1.57	1.53	2.42	5.25		5.76
1973	3.53	4.94	5.85	7.01	1.08	7.25	1.68	4.29	3.76	6.08	6.20	7.40		9.87
1974	5.29	5.64	5.86	2.23	(1.12)	6.71	(4.61)	5.15	(1.24)	3.15	6.32	5.98		12.33
1975	4.70	3.75	6.11	3.21	2.81	6.72	(0.65)	2.59	1.81	2.12	4.36	7.11		10.48
1976	7.37	3.55	5.40	0.33	0.24	8.44	(12.06)	3.47	1.66	2.52	6.58	10.47	6.97	11.10
1977	2.96	1.51	3.66	1.16	(6.14)	4.46	(10.60)	(2.54)	(2.11)	(6.31)	(1.39)	5.88	3.35	8.91
1978	1.72	1.91	3.60	2.45	(4.94)	6.59	(4.43)	(2.95)	0.20	(0.28)	2.11	9.05	7.83	9.01
1979	1.69	1.83	4.07	2.57	(1.52)	6.82	(0.84)	2.55	2.45	2.13	5.81	11.13	7.76	13.70
1980	2.45	3.43	5.34	2.16	(1.72)	6.86	(4.70)	3.96	3.83	1.40	5.26	9.93	4.86	16.30
1981	(3.06)	(4.51)	2.03	(4.38)	(1.97)	1.99	(9.63)	0.61	(4.19)	(1.64)	1.83	4.32	6.02	13.25
1982	(1.22)	(2.50)	3.69	(3.47)	(5.54)	3.56	(10.39)	(3.15)	(6.91)	(1.47)	3.83	6.91	5.06	11.99
1983	0.37	0.44	4.34	(1.15)	(2.42)	4.49	(8.46)	(3.35)	(6.39)	(1.41)	4.19	5.81	3.43	9.82
1984	(0.97)	(1.34)	3.67	(1.84)	(1.50)	4.01	(7.68)	(3.93)	(2.78)	(2.15)	2.95	5.42	3.50	9.54
1985	3.72	2.50	5.63	2.75	2.51	6.69	(1.85)	(0.38)	1.36	(2.12)	5.59	6.94	5.44	12.23
1986	4.00	1.61	5.13	2.45	1.62	6.18	(2.22)	(3.39)	1.40	0.63	5.07	6.46	5.72	10.94
1987	2.43	1.13	4.24	2.50	(0.79)	5.54	(1.49)	(4.96)	0.94	(0.12)	4.84	5.74	5.35	9.73
1988	2.25	0.61	5.39	3.45	1.48	5.83	(0.92)	(3.14)	2.00	0.01	5.24	7.02	5.60	10.10
1989	4.35	1.60	6.18	5.03	4.04	6.48	1.41	2.40	4.30	2.27	6.08	6.55	8.14	13.85

currency years, and out of 242 currency years British exporters selling in currencies would only have had to sell currencies at a discount, at a loss, on 63 occasions out of 242. This means that on 179 occasions out of 242 British exporters could have sold those currencies for delivery and conversion into sterling at a premium and earned an additional margin of profit. In 1976, for example, British exporters invoicing overseas buyers in US dollars could have earned from the sale of dollars to the bank for conversion into sterling in three months, an average additional margin equivalent to 7.37 per cent per annum. On a three months basis that is just under 2 per cent flat on every 90-day invoice. In 1989 the average three months premium on the US dollar was much reduced to 4.35 per cent per annum: The Dutch guilder, Deutschmark, Swiss franc and yen however, were at premiums of 6.18, 6.48, 6.55 and 8.14 per cent per annum respectively. Conversely, importers paying in currencies and covering their positions had to pay a premium on 179 occasions out of 242 and in 1989 they had to pay on average premiums of 6.18, 6.48, 6.55 and 8.14 per cent per annum for payments in guilders, Deutschmarks, Swiss francs and yen.

While a UK exporter selling into Germany in 1989 and invoicing in Deutschmarks could have sold his Deutschmarks to his bank here in Britain for delivery and conversion into sterling in three months and earned himself an additional margin of profit by way of premium equivalent to 6.48 per cent per annum, if he had been invoicing his buyer in Germany in sterling, and assuming that the German buyer understood how the system works any better than the UK seller, he could have bought sterling forward at a discount equivalent to approximately 6.48 per cent per annum. There is no evidence to show, however, that this assumption is correct. On the contrary, all the evidence points to the fact that the German buyer understands it even less than the UK exporter, and this stems from the fact that there is only a limited market in Germany and as a result very few people ever use it. Because neither seller nor the buyer generate the premium/discount by using the forward market it simply goes by default and is lost.

Table 2 shows the premiums which accrued to British exports of £1m to each of the nine countries scheduled over the three years 1987 to 1989 but translated into £s. Exporters should calculate from their own sales to these countries the amount of additional profit they would have made by selling in each of the currencies. For example, annual sales in US dollars to the value of £5m in 1988 with an average period between date of order and date of payment of approximately three months would have yielded £28,125. Annual sales in Deutschmarks to the value of £2m in 1987 but with an average period between date of order and date of payment of six months would have yielded 13,850 × 2 = £27,700 (see note) × 2 = £55,400. These figures should provide sufficient inducement to any exporter who is still selling in sterling to start selling in currencies.

Table 2   Extra profit/increased competitiveness from the use of foreign currencies, 1987–1989

At a cost of only a few telephone calls and with no exchange risk, UK exporters invoicing in the currencies shown below to the value of £1m each per year and with an average period of three months between date of order and date of payment could have earned the approximate amounts shown below by way of forward premium.

	1987 (£)	1988 (£)	1989 (£)	Totals (£)
US dollar	6075	5625	10875	22575
Canadian dollar	2825	1525	4000	8350
Netherlands guilder	10600	13475	15450	39525
Belgian franc	6250	8625	12575	27450
Deutschmark	13850	14575	16200	44625
French franc	2350	5000	10750	18100
Austrian schilling	12100	13100	15200	40400
Swiss franc	14350	17550	16375	48275
Japanese yen	13375	14000	20350	47725
Totals	81775	93475	121775	297025

Note Where the period between date of order and date of payment is six months, the above figures should be multiplied by 2 and for twelve months multiplied by 4.

Conversely, importers who are paying in currencies should do similar calculations in respect of their purchases and they will realise how much it is costing them for the doubtful privilege of paying their suppliers in currency as opposed to sterling. This problem is fully covered in later chapters of the book.

4   Spot Rates of Exchange

In the days of Empire sterling was firmly fixed to the price of gold and all the major currencies at that time were all firmly fixed to sterling. Before the Second World War, however, things had already begun to change and while sterling was having to relinquish its fixed price to gold the US dollar was emerging as the leading international trading currency. At the Bretton Woods conference in 1944 the exchange rate between sterling and the dollar was fixed at \$4 = £1 and as the value of the dollar was already fixed to the price of gold sterling was again fixed to the price of gold albeit indirectly.

As Britain began to dismantle the Empire after the Second World War the realignment of all the major currencies was precipitated and in 1949 sterling was devalued against the US dollar to \$2.80 = £1 with a further devaluation in 1967 to \$2.40 = £1. The politicians at that time were still striving to maintain fixed exchange rates but the pressures were mounting and in 1971 under the Smithsonian Agreement the dollar was devalued against the price of gold and many of the major currencies were devalued against the dollar and a last stand was made to maintain a system of fixed exchange rates. This did not last, however, and from then on there was a gradual breakdown of fixed exchange rates until finally they were allowed to float and find their own levels in a free market.

All that is meant by floating exchange rates is that the price of any one currency against any other currency, i.e. the exchange rate, is going up and down all day and every day and reacting to political and economic events everywhere in the world in exactly the same way as the price of shares react on the stock exchanges. A 'spot' rate of exchange, therefore, is the rate of exchange now, this moment. In actual deals however, this will normally entail two working days.

The figures set out in Table 3 have been extracted from the *Financial Times* which provides the only comprehensive daily cover of London's exchange and interest rates. These are obtained from a number of different sources and should only be taken therefore as an indication of the previous day's rates. In Table 3 you will see two columns the *Day's spread* and *Close*. In the *Day's spread* column there are two rates shown; two figures against each country. These figures do not reflect buying or selling although there is a slight difference between buying and selling at the spot rate which constitutes the bank's profit. The figures merely reflect the range of the fluctuations of the spot rate during the course of the previous day, in other words if you look alongside US for dollars you will see figures 1.5340 and 1.5460. These are not buying and selling figures but merely an indication that the spot rate of the dollar against sterling during the course of that day fluctuated between $1.5340 and $1.5460. For record purposes, therefore, it is suggested you take the mid-point of the day's spread, i.e. 1.5400. Similarly, the mid-point of the day's spread for the West German mark against sterling is 3.0700. The column headed 'Close' indicates the difference between buying and selling at the spot rate at the close of business.

Table 3   Pound spot – forward against pound, 11 September 1989

	Day's spread	Close	One month		% p.a.	Three months		% p.a.
US	1.5340–1.5460	1.5450–1.5460	0.64–0.61c	PM	4.85	1.86–1.82	PM	4.76
Canada	1.8265–1.8375	1.8330–1.8340	0.29–0.20c	PM	1.60	0.78–0.65	PM	1.56
Netherlands	3.45¼–3.46¾	3.45½–3.46½	1⅞–1¾	PM	6.29	5⅜–5⅛	PM	6.07
Belgium	64.10–64.45	64.25–64.35	31–27c	PM	5.41	86–81	PM	5.19
Denmark	11.90¾–11.95	11.93½–11.94½	4¾–4⅜ Ore	PM	4.59	12⅞–12⅛	PM	4.19
Ireland	1.1460–1.1520	1.1500–1.1510	0.40–0.35c	PM	3.91	1.10–1.00	PM	3.65
West Germany	3.06½–3.07½	3.06½–3.07½	1¾–1⅜pf	PM	6.11	4⅞–4¾	PM	6.27
Portugal	255.80–257.20	256.15–257.15	24–6c		0.70	12–29 Dis		–0.32
Spain	190.95–192.10	191.40–191.70	14–22 c Dis		–1.13	26–42 Dis		–0.71
Italy	2197½–2206	2200¼–2201¼	5–3 Lire	PM	2.18	10–8	PM	1.64
Norway	11.14½–11.18½	11.17¼–11.18¼	2⅞–2⅜ Ore	PM	2.82	8⅜–7⅞	PM	2.91
France	10.33–10.37	10.33¾–10.34¾	4⅛–4 c	PM	4.71	11⅞–11⅝	PM	4.54
Sweden	10.32–10.35	10.33¾–10.34¾	1⅞–1¾ Ore	PM	2.10	5⅝–5¼	PM	2.10
Japan	226¾–227¾	226½–227½	1⅝–1½ yen	PM	8.26	4½–4⅜	PM	7.82
Austria	21.59–21.68	21.59–21.62	12⅝–11⅝ Gro	PM	6.73	35¾–33	PM	6.36
Switzerland	2.64½–2.65¾	2.64½–2.65½	1⅜–1¼ c	PM	5.94	4⅛–4	PM	6.13
ECU	1.4745–1.4760	1.4750–1.4760	0.54–0.51c	PM	4.27	1.47–1.42	PM	3.92

Abbreviations: PM = premium, Dis = discount, c = cent, pf = pfennig,
Gro = gröschen, % p.a. = per cent per annum.

5 Selling and Buying Currencies Forward

Assuming now that a UK exporter has gone to the USA and has sold a product to the value of £10,000 and has converted that £10,000 into dollars at a rate of exchange of $1.5400 = £1. That means that he has now an order for $15,400 which he expects to receive say in about one month or three months time. If he had the dollars today and converted them back into sterling at $1.5400 he would have £10,000. But of course he is not going to receive the dollars today, he is going to receive them in say either one month or three months time. What then will be the value of those dollars in sterling terms when he receives them in one month or three months time? Here you have the problem. He has got an order but of course he has no knowledge at all of what that order will be worth in sterling terms when he receives the dollars.

In order to overcome this problem therefore the exporter rings up his bank and says, 'I will sell you $15,400 today and I will undertake to *deliver* $15,400 on or about day 30, 60, 90, whenever'. He would not normally undertake to deliver those dollars on day 90 because he is not sure he is going to receive them on day 90. He would invariably give himself some days of grace, a period during which he can deliver those dollars. This period is called an 'option'.

If the exporter was expecting to receive his $15,400 in about three months time he might undertake to deliver them to the bank any day between day 90 and day 120, in other words he is giving himself a month in which to deliver those dollars. Nevertheless this is a firm undertaking by the exporter to the bank to deliver $15,400 any working day between day 90 and day 120. If the currency is at a premium the exporter will earn the premium calculated to the earliest date, i.e. day 90 in the above example, if

31

the currency is at a discount the exporter will pay the discount calculated to the latest date, i.e. day 120. In the case of imports it is vice versa. The importer will earn the discount calculated to the earliest date and pay the premium calculated to the latest date.

Up to this point it has not cost the exporter anything except the telephone call. He has merely made a commitment to deliver the dollars. In exchange for the exporter's undertaking to deliver the dollars any day between day 90 and day 120, the bank will fix the rate today at which it will convert those dollars back into sterling when the exporter delivers them any day between day 90 and day 120. This is called the 'forward rate'; a rate of exchange agreed today, at which a bank will convert currency either on a future date or between two future dates and whatever the spot rate happens to be at the time the bank is firmly committed to convert those dollars back into sterling at the agreed forward rate.

If you will now look at the 'One month' and 'Three months' columns in Table 3 you will see two figures in each of those columns. Alongside US for dollars in the 'One month' column you will see 0.64, 0.61c for cents and PM for premium. In the 'Three months' column you will see 1.86, 1.82 PM for premium. These mean that both the one month and three months forward dollar are at a premium against sterling. The greater figure in both these columns, i.e. 0.64 and 1.86 is always the importing figure, and the lesser figure, i.e. 0.61 and 1.82 is always the exporting figure: namely, if you are buying you pay a higher price and if you are selling you receive a lower price. The difference reflects the bank's profit on the deal.

Whereas the two figures in the 'Days's spread' column do not reflect buying and selling but are simply an indication of the fluctuations in the spot rate during the course of the day, the figures in the 'One month' and 'Three months' columns do reflect buying and selling. Be very careful, however. You may be buying but the bank is selling and you have no idea how many people end up by buying instead of selling or selling instead of buying. So, in order to avoid the confusion think of them as importing and exporting. Obviously, if you are importing you are buying the currency in order to pay for the goods. If you are exporting and receiving the currency you are selling that currency to the bank to have it converted back into sterling.

Assume that you are importing and you have now placed an order for $15,400 on a US supplier and you are going to have to pay in about one month's time. The same arguments apply in so far that no one knows how much sterling you will have to pay for those dollars in one month. There is no law that says that you cannot buy them today at a rate of exchange of $1.5400 = £1 and put them on deposit until you require them. They will earn a certain amount of interest but you might have better things to do with your money. So you buy the dollars forward and say to the bank, 'I will buy $15,400 today and I will undertake to *take up delivery* of those dollars on or about day 30, 60, 90 whenever'. If you were undertaking to take up delivery of the dollars on about day 30 then you would buy them at a premium of 0.64c. If you were taking up delivery of the dollars in about three months time you would buy them at a premium of 1.86c. Now you are buying the currency at a premium and increasing the cost of your purchase. If you do not know exactly when during the next 30 or 90 days you will be requiring the currency, you can buy it forward with an open option. In this case you would pay the premium of 0.64c and be able to take delivery any day between days 1 and 30. Similarly, by paying the premium of 1.86c you could take delivery any day between days 1 and 90. If the currency was at a discount and you wanted to take delivery between days 1 and 30 or 90, you would forfeit your discount and pay the spot rate current at the time you transacted the forward contract for the full period of the thirty or ninety days.

If on the other hand you are exporting, receiving the dollars in about one month's time and delivering them to the bank in about one month's time, then you would be selling the dollars at a premium of 0.61c. If you were delivering the dollars to the bank in about three months time you would be selling them to the bank at a premium of 1.82c, and because you are selling at a premium you will be making more money. If you wanted to deliver the currency to the bank any day between days 1 and 30 or 90 you would forfeit the premium and be paid at the spot rate current when you transacted the forward contract for the full period of thirty or ninety days.

'Do you want it fixed or option?' is a question with which exporters and importers very often are faced, and they should be wary before replying. 'Do you want it fixed?' is easy enough. It means, do you want to deliver currency to the bank or take up delivery of currency from the bank on a fixed date? But what does the bank mean by do you want it option? It could mean do you want to deliver or take up delivery of the currency between two future dates or it could mean, do you want to deliver or take up delivery of the currency any day between days 1 and 30 or 90 in which event you are going to forfeit the premium if you are selling or discount if you are buying forward. The answer to the question 'Do you want it fixed or option?' is usually 'neither, we will deliver or take up delivery of the currency between that date and that date'.

With further reference to Table 3, the two columns headed % p.a. show the premiums and discounts as rates per cent per annum and these will be explained in greater detail during later stages of the book.

6 Calculating Premiums and Discounts

In calculating the forward rate of exchange a premium is always *subtracted* from the spot rate and a discount is always *added* to the spot rate, par indicates that there is no premium and no discount and so the forward rate will be the same as the spot rate. In accordance with Figure 1 below if you had been exporting and delivering the dollars to the bank in about one month's time, you would have sold them at a premium of 0.61 cents. Because this is a premium, it is a minus quantity and you subtract 0.61 cent from 54.00 cents. Be very careful of that point, the spot rate is one dollar 54.00 cents and the premium is 0.61 cents. The one month forward rate for exports is therefore $1.5339 = £1. If you had been delivering the dollars in about three months you would have sold them to the bank at a premium of 1.82 cents resulting in a forward rate of $1.5218 = £1. Against the spot rate $1.5400, at which you converted your sterling price into dollars, the premiums of 0.61 cent and 1.82 cents would have yielded an extra £40 and £120 respectively at a cost of only a phone call. You would have fixed the sterling price of that dollar sale at the time you made the sale which is what you would have done if you had

Figure 1

Spot $1.5400 = £1 ∴ $15,400 = £10,000

PREMIUM 1 MONTH 0.61c

Forward rate $1.5339 ∴ $15,400 = £10,040

PREMIUM 3 MONTHS 1.82c

Forward rate $1.5218 ∴ $15,400 = £10,120

sold in sterling but you have now made more profit. You do not have to try and guess as to what the order will bring in. The exchange rate is fixed and that is the end of the sale.

Some people might be tempted not to sell the dollars forward at the time of receiving an order in the hope that the exchange rate would go in their favour and that they could sell them to the bank at the spot rate when the dollars came in and thus end up in three months time receiving more than £10,000. On the other hand they could just as easily end up by receiving far less than £10,000. If the sterling price can be fixed at the outset and provide an additional margin of profit into the bargain, there seems little justification in running the exchange risk.

In the case of an importer wishing to take up delivery of dollars in about one month Figure 2 shows that he would have paid a premium of 0.64 cents which he subtracted from the spot rate of $1.5400, arriving at a forward rate of $1.5336 = £1. Similarly, if he was taking up delivery of the dollars in about three months he would have subtracted 1.86 cents from the spot rate arriving at a forward rate of $1.5214 = £1. He would thus have had to pay not £10,000 but £10,042 and £10,122 respectively. Similarly to the exporter above, the buyer might be tempted not to buy the dollars forward at the time of placing the order on his supplier but to wait and buy them at the spot rate when payment was due in the hope that the exchange rate would go in his favour. Equally, he might be disappointed.

Figure 2

Spot $1.5400 = £1 ∴ $15,400 = £10,000

PREMIUM 1 MONTH 0.64c

Forward $1.5336 = £10,042

PREMIUM 3 MONTHS 1.86c

Forward $1.5214 = £10,122

Figure 3 envisages an export sale in Deutschmarks with payment in either one or three months. The exporter can sell the Deutschmarks forward to his bank in the UK for conversion into sterling in one or three months and either make himself an additional £45 or £157 profit or reduce the Deutschmark price of his product by the Deutschmark equivalent of £45 or £157. If he had sold those goods to the German for £10,000 sterling however, and assuming that the German understands the technology better than the British exporter, he could have bought the sterling forward at a discount and reduced his purchase price by the equivalent of £45 or £157. If neither party had sold or bought forward, that £45 or £157 would simply have gone by default. It is there to be had but it has to be generated by either one party or the other.

Figure 3

Spot DM3.0700 = £1 ∴ DM30,700 = £10,000

PREMIUM 1 MONTH 1.37pf

Forward DM3.0563 ∴ DM30,700 = £10,045

PREMIUM 3 MONTHS 4.75pf

Forward DM3.0225 ∴ DM30.700 = £10,157

Exercise

With the help of Figures 3, 4 and 5 and the extract from the *Financial Times* in Table 3, exporters should now calculate one and three months rates in Deutschmarks, pesetas and yen. The advantages of selling in Deutschmarks and yen will be self-evident, and although the peseta is at a discount, from a marketing viewpoint it is still better to sell in pesetas as the distributor will otherwise load his peseta prices by a much higher margin than the amount of the discount. This facet of marketing is dealt with in later chapters.

Figure 4

Spot Peseta 191.525 = £1 ∴ Peseta 1,915,250 = £10,000

DISCOUNT 1 MONTH 22c

Forward Peseta 191.745 = £1 ∴ Peseta 1,915,250 = £9,989

DISCOUNT 3 MONTHS 42c

Forward Peseta 191.945 = £1 ∴ Peseta 1,915,250 = £9,978

Figure 5

Spot Yen 227.25 = £1 ∴ yen 2,272,500 = £10,000

PREMIUM 1 MONTH 1.5 yen

Forward Yen 225.75 = £1 ∴ yen 2,272,500 = £10,066

PREMIUM 3 MONTHS 4.375 yen

Forward Yen 222.875 = £1 ∴ yen 2,272,500 = £10,196

With the help of Figures 6 and 7 and with reference to Table 3, importers should calculate the one and three months rates in Deutschmarks and pesetas.

Figure 6

Spot DM3.0700 = £1 ∴ DM30,700 = £10,000

PREMIUM 1 MONTH 1.75pf

Forward DM3,0525 = £10,057

PREMIUM 3 MONTHS 4.875pf

Forward DM3.02125 = £10,161

Figure 7

Spot Peseta 191.525 = £1 ∴ Peseta 1,915,250 = £10,000

DISCOUNT 1 MONTH 14c

Forward rate 191.665 = £1 ∴ Peseta 1,915,250 = £9,993

DISCOUNT 3 MONTHS 26c

Forward rate 191.785 = £1 ∴ Pesta 1,915,250 = £9,986

---

7 What is a Forward Rate?

A forward rate in no way reflects what the bank thinks the spot rate is likely to be at some future date. No foreign exchange dealer is in the guessing game, and in order to understand the reason why this is the case one has to refer back to the days when the Euro-currency market was being established in London. At that time no country had ever set out to establish a money market of this kind and consequently no one knew what the ground rules for running such a market should be. The banks in London therefore looked to the Bank of England in order to conceive a set of ground rules on which such a market should operate. After several months they came up with an appropriate set of rules within which the Bank of England insisted on the observance of the 'golden rule' principle that no bank should speculate in currencies.

In practical terms this means that banks have to close out their positions in currency at the end of each day and they do this by way of borrowing or lending the currency concerned in the Euro-currency market against a lending or borrowing of the other currency involved, i.e. Euro-sterling if converting into or out of sterling. The premium or the discount is therefore based on the difference in Euro-currency interest rates. The figures set out in Table 4 have been extracted from the *Financial Times*.

If a bank has bought or sold currency today for delivery or receipt at some time in the future, it covers itself by setting up the deal today. In the event of the exporter selling Deutschmarks to the bank for delivery in three months, in order to close out its position on the same day the bank will borrow the Euro-Deutschmarks for a fixed period of three months at a fixed rate of 7¼ per cent per annum (7.2500). See also Figure 8.

Table 4 Euro-currency interest rates

11 September 1989

	Short-term	7 days notice	One month	Three months	Six months	One year
Sterling	$13^{13}/_{16}$–$13^{11}/_{16}$	$13^{7}/_{8}$–$13^{3}/_{4}$	$13^{15}/_{16}$–$13^{7}/_{8}$	14–$13^{15}/_{16}$	14–$13^{7}/_{8}$	$13^{3}/_{4}$–$13^{11}/_{16}$
US dollar	$8^{7}/_{8}$–$8^{3}/_{4}$	$8^{15}/_{16}$–$8^{13}/_{16}$	9–$8^{7}/_{8}$	$8^{15}/_{16}$–$8^{13}/_{16}$	$8^{15}/_{16}$–$8^{13}/_{16}$	$8^{15}/_{16}$–$8^{13}/_{16}$
Canadian dollar	$11^{7}/_{8}$–$11^{5}/_{8}$	$11^{7}/_{8}$–$11^{5}/_{8}$	$12^{1}/_{16}$–$11^{11}/_{16}$	$12^{1}/_{16}$–$11^{11}/_{16}$	$11^{15}/_{16}$–$11^{11}/_{16}$	$11^{13}/_{16}$–$11^{9}/_{16}$
Dutch guilder	$7^{3}/_{8}$–$7^{1}/_{8}$	$7^{3}/_{8}$–$7^{1}/_{8}$	$7^{7}/_{16}$–$7^{5}/_{16}$	$7^{1}/_{2}$–$7^{3}/_{8}$	$7^{9}/_{16}$–$7^{7}/_{16}$	$7^{5}/_{8}$–$7^{1}/_{2}$
Swiss franc	$7^{5}/_{8}$–$7^{1}/_{2}$	$7^{5}/_{8}$–$7^{1}/_{2}$	$7^{5}/_{8}$–$7^{1}/_{2}$	$7^{5}/_{8}$–$7^{1}/_{2}$	$7^{5}/_{8}$–$7^{1}/_{2}$	$7^{7}/_{16}$–$7^{5}/_{16}$
Deutschmark	$7^{3}/_{16}$–$7^{1}/_{16}$	$7^{3}/_{16}$–$7^{1}/_{16}$	$7^{3}/_{16}$–$7^{1}/_{16}$	$7^{3}/_{8}$–$7^{1}/_{4}$	$7^{7}/_{16}$–$7^{5}/_{16}$	$7^{7}/_{16}$–$7^{5}/_{16}$
French franc	$9^{1}/_{16}$–$8^{15}/_{16}$	$9^{1}/_{16}$–$8^{15}/_{16}$	$9^{1}/_{8}$–9	$9^{1}/_{4}$–$9^{1}/_{8}$	$9^{1}/_{4}$–$9^{1}/_{8}$	$9^{1}/_{4}$–$9^{1}/_{8}$
Italian lire	12–10	$11^{1}/_{4}$–$10^{1}/_{4}$	12–$11^{1}/_{2}$	$12^{1}/_{4}$–$11^{3}/_{4}$	$12^{3}/_{8}$–12	$12^{1}/_{2}$–$12^{1}/_{8}$
Belgian franc (fin)	$8^{3}/_{16}$–$8^{1}/_{16}$	$8^{3}/_{8}$–$8^{1}/_{4}$	$8^{1}/_{2}$–$8^{3}/_{8}$	$8^{11}/_{16}$–$8^{9}/_{16}$	$8^{11}/_{16}$–$8^{9}/_{16}$	$8^{11}/_{16}$–$8^{9}/_{16}$
Belgian franc (con)	$8^{1}/_{4}$–$7^{7}/_{8}$	$8^{1}/_{2}$–$8^{1}/_{8}$	$8^{5}/_{8}$–$8^{1}/_{4}$	$8^{13}/_{16}$–$8^{7}/_{16}$	$8^{13}/_{16}$–$8^{7}/_{16}$	$8^{13}/_{16}$–$8^{7}/_{16}$
Yen	$5^{3}/_{8}$–$5^{1}/_{4}$	$5^{7}/_{16}$–$5^{5}/_{16}$	$5^{3}/_{4}$–$5^{5}/_{8}$	$5^{3}/_{4}$–$5^{5}/_{8}$	$5^{3}/_{4}$–$5^{5}/_{8}$	$5^{3}/_{4}$–$5^{5}/_{8}$
D. Krone	$9^{3}/_{16}$–$9^{1}/_{16}$	$9^{3}/_{16}$–$9^{1}/_{16}$	$9^{5}/_{16}$–$9^{1}/_{4}$	$9^{1}/_{2}$–$9^{7}/_{16}$	$9^{5}/_{8}$–$9^{1}/_{2}$	$9^{3}/_{4}$–$9^{5}/_{8}$
Asian $ (Sing.)	$8^{15}/_{16}$–$8^{13}/_{16}$	9–$8^{7}/_{8}$	9–$8^{7}/_{8}$	9–$8^{7}/_{8}$	$8^{15}/_{16}$–$8^{13}/_{16}$	$8^{7}/_{8}$–$8^{3}/_{4}$

Long term Euro-dollars: two years $8^{15}/_{16}$–$8^{13}/_{16}$ per cent; three years $8^{15}/_{16}$–$8^{13}/_{16}$ per cent; four years $8^{15}/_{16}$–$8^{13}/_{16}$ per cent; five years $8^{15}/_{16}$–$8^{13}/_{16}$ per cent nominal. Short-term rates are call for US $ and yen; others two days notice.

The Bank will then convert the Deutschmarks into sterling and lend the Euro-sterling for the same period at a fixed rate of 14 per cent per annum (14.0000). The bank is therefore making a profit of 6.7500 per cent per annum and it is this profit which the bank passes on to the exporter by way of premium. The bank's profit on the deal is reflected in the difference in the interest rates at which it borrows and lends and this is measured by the difference in the premium for importing and exporting, i.e. 4⅞ and 4¾pf. As we are looking at the three months forward rate we divide the difference between the borrowing and lending rates by 4 to get a flat rate per cent of 1.6875. 1.6875 per cent of the spot rate DM3.0700 = DM0.0518, which is 5.18pf.

Figure 8   Premium – discount difference in Euro-currency interest rates.

Lend   3 months   £ @ 14.0000% p.a.
Borrow 3 months DM @ 7.2500% p.a.

Difference   6.7500% p.a.
÷ 4 = 1.68750% flat

1.6875% of DM3.0700 = DM0.0518
Premium 5.18pf

Referring back to Table 3, the column headed % p.a. shows the difference in interest rates as 6.27 per cent per annum and the three months forward premium for exports as 4¾pf (4.75pf). Well, the published rates are only an indication and constitute an average over a number of banks and so the sums rarely if ever work out exactly alike. If you were to get the premium and the interest rates from the same bank they would of course work out exactly because that in effect is how the bank itself has calculated the premium.

In the case shown in Figure 3 the bank has covered itself by virtue of the fact that it has a liability by way of a borrowing of DM30,700 and an asset by way of a receivable from the exporter of DM30,700, and it has established the cost of the transaction at the outset. Moreover, at the time the bank has to repay the loan of DM30,700 the exporter is due to deliver DM30,700 and the bank is therefore not incurring any exchange risk. What happens if the exporter cannot deliver on time is dealt with in Chapter 9, 'Extending a forward contract'.

In the case shown in Figure 9, regarding an import from Italy, the buyer is going to have to pay lire 22.0175m in three months time. He has therefore bought the lire today and is going to take up delivery in three months time. By the end of today the bank will lend lire 22.0175m for three months at an interest rate of 12¼ per cent per annum (12.2500) against borrowing sterling for three months at 13¹⁵⁄₁₆ per cent per annum (13.9375). The difference between the two interest rates is 1.6875 per cent per annum. Divided by four as we are calculating the three months' premium, the answer is 0.421875 per cent flat. 0.421875 per cent of the spot rate lire 2201.75 = lire 9.29. Subtract lire 9.29 from lire 2201.75 and the forward rate is lire 2192.46 = £1.

Figure 9   Premium – discount difference in Euro-currency interest rates.

Borrow 3 months sterling @ 13.9375% p.a.
Lend   3 months lire   @ 12.2500% p.a.

Difference	1.6875% p.a.
÷ by 4	= 0.421875% flat

0.421875% of spot lire 2201.75 = lire 9.29

Premium 9.29 lire

The bank is losing money and this is the premium which it will charge to the importer. At the end of the three months period the bank will receive those lire so that it will have the lire to pass on to the importer. Again the bank has a balanced position with a liability to the importer of lire 22.0175m and an asset by way of a loan of lire 22.0175m. Moreover, it has no exchange risk as it will not have to buy the lire in three months time.

The bank's risk in a forward transaction arises when the exporter or importer cannot meet his obligation and has to close out the contract. In the event of a loss the bank's concern is 'can he afford to pay?' The bank is not at risk for the principal, unless it is funding the credit, but only for the difference in the forward and spot rates. It will usually protect itself against this risk by calculating up to 20 per cent of each forward transaction and arranging a cumulative limit up to which they will transact forward contracts.

We have assumed so far that the exporter and/or the importer is British and has to reconcile his debtors and creditors from a sterling base. The exporter who is selling in currency therefore wishes to fix the rate at which his currency receivables will be converted back into sterling at some time in the future. Similarly, the importer wishes to fix the rate at which his bank will convert sterling into currency at some time in the future.

This does not mean, however, that either cannot convert currencies into other currencies than sterling. The exporter for example, may sell forward in order to fix the rate at which his Deutschmarks receivables will be converted back into US dollars. In this case, the bank will close out its position by borrowing Euro-Deutschmarks against lending Euro-dollars and calculating the premium in exactly the same way. Similarly, if the importer happens to be the UK subsidiary of an American parent for example, and is working from a US dollar base, he may buy lire forward and fix the rate at which his bank will convert US dollars into lire at some time in the future. In this case the bank will close out its position by lending Euro-lire against borrowing Euro-dollars and calculate the discount accordingly.

Exercise

With the help of Table 4 and Figures 10 and 11 calculate the six months forward exporting rate against sterling for Deutschmarks and the six months forward importing rate for lire.

Figure 10 Premium – discount difference in Euro-currency interest rates.

Lend   6 months £   @ 14.0000% p.a.
Borrow 6 months DM @   7.3125% p.a.

Difference   6.6875% p.a.
÷ by 2   = 3.34375% flat

3.34375% of DM3.0700 = DM0.1027

Premium 10.27pf

Forward rate DM spot 3.0700 − 10.27pf =
DM2.9673 = £1

Figure 11 Premium – discount difference in Euro-currency interest rates.

Borrow 6 months £   @ 13.8750% p.a.
Lend   6 months lire @ 12.3750% p.a.

Difference   1.5000% p.a.
÷ by 2   = 0.7500% flat

0.7500% of lire 2201.75 = lire 16.51

Premium 16.51 lire

Forward rate lire spot 2201.75 − 16.51 =
lire 2185.24 = £1

8 Monitoring Euro-currency Interest Rates

The reason why it is so essential for both exporters and importers to understand how the forward market works is to ensure that they monitor the Euro-currency interest rates. Whereas the spot rate may well be gyrating up and down in a very erratic fashion and while the interest rates do change, they do not move anything like as erratically as the spot rate can move. They therefore provide a much more stable factor, and it is the difference in Euro-currency interest rates that requires to be monitored rather than the spot rate because these will show variations in the premiums and/or discounts, which in turn can be projected much more safely. For example, in order to brief a sales executive who may be setting out on an overseas trip lasting a month, it is of much greater practical help for him to know that however much the spot rate happens to move during that period he will still have an additional margin by way of forward premium of x per cent with which to negotiate. To provide him with a fictitious rate based on someone's guess as to what the spot rate is likely to be might well have unfortunate results. See Figure 12 for 1988 and 1989.

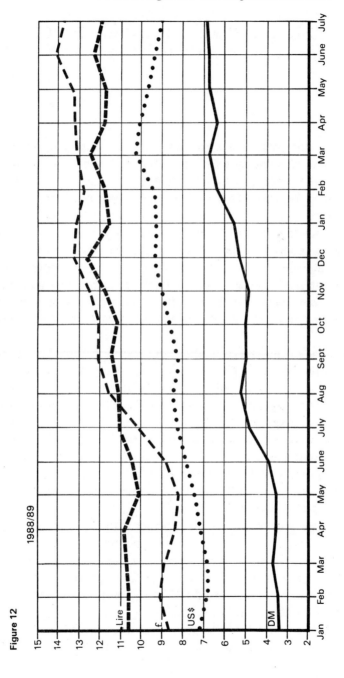

Figure 12

1988/89

9 Extending a Forward Contract

One of the great bogys in most people's minds about selling currency forward is what happens if, having undertaken to deliver the currency in say about three months time, you cannot deliver it because the buyer is late in paying. This does not necessarily present a problem. You nevertheless have to meet your commitment to deliver the currency and as you are not going to receive the currency from the overseas buyer you have to go into the open market and buy it at the spot rate in order to close out your contract with the bank. This may cost you money or you may make money depending on what the spot rate has done in relation to your original conversion rate and forward rate.

Figure 13 shows a case where an exporter received an order in March for $14,622 with payment due in June. Against a spot rate of $1.4622 = £1 he sold the dollars forward for delivery and conversion in June at a rate of $1.4475. There was a substantial delay in delivery and consequently payment. The exporter therefore had to close out his forward contract. He brought dollars at the current spot rate of $1.5072 and they only cost him £9701, making him a profit of £299 against his original conversion rate. He did, however, still make his premium of £101 and his overall gain was therefore £400.

Having now closed out his contract with the bank he sold the dollar receivables forward again to the new anticipated date of receipt and the new forward rate of $1.4975 was geared to the new spot rate of $1.5072. When he subsequently delivered the dollars they were converted at $1.4975 and only yielded £9764, thereby showing him a loss of £236.

Figure 14 shows a case where the spot rate has gone against him when he comes to close out his contract and he has made a

Figure 13

Extending forward: contract £10,000

March		June	
Spot	3 months	Spot	3 months
$1.4622	$1.4475	$1.5072	$1.4975
$14,622	£10,101	£9.701	£9,764
		Gain	Loss
		£299	£236
	+ Premium	£101	
	Total gain	£400	

Figure 14

Extending forward: contract £10,000

March		June	
Spot	3 months	Spot	3 months
$1.4622	$1.4475	$1.4425	$1.4275
$14,622	£10,101	£10,137	£10,243
		Loss	Gain
		£137	£243
	− Premium	£101	
	Net loss	£ 36	

---

loss of £137 in buying the dollars spot. He still makes the premium of £101, however, and so his net loss is £36. On selling the receivables forward again to the new anticipated date of receipt he makes a gain of £243.

In Figure 15 the exporter has sold the dollars forward at a discount of £102 and when he buys the dollars in June at the spot rate he makes a further loss of £137 as the spot rate has gone against him. Moreover, when he eventually delivers the dollars

Figure 15

Extending forward: contract £10,000

	March		June	
Spot	3 months	Spot	3 months
$1.4622	$1.4772	$1.4425	$1.4675
$14,622	£9,898	£10,137	£9,964
		Loss	Loss
		£137	£36
	+ Discount	£102	
	Total loss	£239	

---

he will make another loss of £36 because the new forward rate is still at a discount.

Figure 16 shows the reverse position where a buyer has bought dollars forward for payment to an overseas supplier in three months. This will cost him a premium of £104. If he has to delay payment, however, and sell the dollars back to the bank at the spot rate of $1.5072 in order to close out his contract he will only receive £9701 and thereby make a loss of £299. He will still have

Figure 16

Extending forward contract £10,000

	March		June	
Spot	3 months	Spot	3 months
$1.4622	$1.4471	$1.5072	$1.4970
$14,622	£10,104	£9,701	£9,768
		Loss	Gain
		£299	£232
	+ Premium	£104	
	Total loss	£403	

---

to pay the premium of £104, however, making a total loss of £403. On buying the dollars forward again for payment at the new anticipated date he will purchase them at $1.4970 which will cost him only £9768 thus providing a gain of £232.

In Figure 17 the importer will gain £137 when closing out his contract but will have to pay the premium of £109 reducing his gain to £28. He will lose £250 when buying again at the new anticipated date.

Figure 17

Extending forward contract £10,000

	March			June	
Spot	3 months		Spot	3 months	
$1.4622	$1.4465		$1.4425	$1.4265	
$14,622	£10,109		£10,137	£10,250	
			Gain	Loss	
			£137	£250	
	− Premium		£109		
	Net gain		£ 28		

In Figure 18 the buyer has bought the dollars forward at a discount of £102 but when he sells them back to the bank to close out his contract the spot rate has gone in his favour and he will make a further gain of £137 making a total gain of £239. Moreover, the new forward rate is also at a discount and he will make a further gain of £36.

If it is a question of having to close out the forward contract because you are never going to receive the currency due to the buyer's bankruptcy, then you have to buy the currency at the spot rate and you will either win or lose depending on the new spot rate compared with your original conversion and forward rates. The same will apply to the importer who has to close out his forward contract. If the exporter insures with ECGD,

Figure 18

Extending forward: contract £10,000

March		June	
Spot	3 months	Spot	3 months
$1.4622	$1.4772	$1.4425	$1.4675
$14,622	£9,898	£10,137	£9,964
		Gain	Gain
		£137	£36
	+ Discount	£102	
	Total gain	£239	

---

however, and incurs a loss covered by his policy, the additional loss which he may suffer by having to close out a forward contract may also be covered.

While the book speaks of buying or selling the currency in order to close out a forward contract followed by selling or buying forward again to the new anticipated date of receipt or payment, in practice the two transactions are combined into one. They have been split to help the reader's understanding.

As Figures 13 to 18 have shown, the need to extend a forward contract does not necessarily spell disaster. While accepting that anything can happen, it is important to remember that premiums and discounts are only reflections of the differences in interest rates and that while they can and do move they do not normally move catastrophically. Any alarmist who predicts that the Deutschmark, for example, can go from a premium to a discount against sterling overnight is virtually saying that the Euro-Deutschmark interest rates can go from 7 per cent per annum to 13 per cent per annum overnight, or that Euro-sterling can drop from 13 per cent per annum to 7 per cent per annum.

10   Currency Options

This kind of option should not be confused with the 'option' period contained in a forward contract which provides days of grace for delivery or taking up delivery of currency. It is a relatively new facility now available in the City of London. The benefit of a currency option against selling currency forward or buying currency forward is that it gives the purchaser of the option the right, but not the obligation, to buy or sell currency at a fixed rate on or before the agreed date. This enables a trader to fix a rate of exchange at some time in the future, up to twelve months normally, and gives him the option of taking up that exchange rate if the current spot rate has gone against him. On the other hand, if the current spot rate has gone in his favour he does not have to meet any obligations as he would under a forward contract, but merely does not take up the option although of course he has had to pay the fee known as the premium but again not to be confused with the premium arising from a forward contract.

'Traded', 'exchange' or 'listed' options are those quoted on a recognized exchange such as the London International Financial Futures Exchange (LIFFE) or the London Stock Exchange. These contracts are highly standardised, each having a fixed size and a range of specified strike prices and expiry dates.

'Over the counter' options are written by a number of leading banks and are available in most major currencies. They are more flexible and can be tailored to an individual customer's needs.

The factors which determine the premium (fee) are as follows:

1. Maturity – the time to expiry of the option during which period the holder may wish to exercise the option.
2. The strike price – the specified exchange rate at which the

holder of the option can exercise his right to buy or sell a currency during the option period.

3. Spot and forward exchange rates prevailing for the currency of the option contract, at the date of taking out the option.
4. Whether the option is American or European. (See Glossary.)
5. Volatility – the expected fluctuation of the exchange rate of the option currency over the life of the option.
6. The return on investing the premium.

Figure 19 illustrates a case where an exporter bought an option with a strike price of $1.40. When he came to exchange the $1m receivables the dollar had strengthened to $1.30 and so he let the option lapse and converted at the spot rate. After deducting the premium (fee) the net yield was £744,945. This yield shows a better result than was likely through a forward sale.

Figure 19

$1m receivable due in 3 months
Spot $1.40 = £1 – $ rises to 1.30 = £1
Let option lapse – deal at spot

Yield at 1.30	£769,231
– Fee @ 3.4% ($34,000)	24,286
Net yield	744,945
Yield @ forward: say 1.39	£719,424

Figure 20 shows an opposite situation where the dollar had weakened to $1.50 and the exporter therefore took up the option and converted the dollars at $1.40. The net yield in this case was only £690,000 whereas a forward sale of the dollars may well have yielded more, say £719,424.

Figure 20

$1m receivable due in 3 months
Spot $1.40 = £1 – $ falls to 1.50 = £1
Exercise option to buy £ at 1.40

Yield at 1.40	£714,286
– Fee @ 3.4% ($34,000)	24,286
Net yield	£690,000
Yield @ forward: say 1.39	£719,424

Figure 21 illustrates the case of an importer with a payable of $1m who buys an option with a strike price of $1.40. When he came to pay the account the dollar had weakened to $1.50. He therefore let the option lapse and dealt at the spot rate. After paying the premium the gross cost was £690,953 whereas if he had bought the dollars forward it could have cost him more.

Figure 21

$1m payable due in 3 months
Spot $1.40 = £1 – $ falls to 1.50 = £1
Let option lapse – deal at spot

Cost at 1.50	£666,667
+ Fee @ 3.4% ($34,000)	24,286
Gross cost	£690,953
Cost @ forward: say 1.39	£719,424

Figure 22 shows the reverse situation when the dollar had strengthened to $1.30 and so he exercised the option to buy at $1.40. With the premium this cost him £738,572 whereas he might have been able to buy the dollars forward at a lower price.

Figure 22

$1m payable due in 3 months
Spot $1.40 = £1 – $ rises to 1.30 = £1
Exercise option to buy £ at 1.40

Cost at 1.40	£714,286
+ Fee @ 3.4% ($34,000)	24,286
Gross cost	£738,572
Cost @ forward: say 1.39	£719,424

These examples have been quoted by a leading London bank although the premiums may have altered since the quotation was given.

Currency options represent one means of protection from exchange risks. They do not necessarily always represent the best method available and other means of covering currency exposure should also be considered. They can be very useful however, particularly when there is a need to cover contingent liabilities such as when tendering for large export orders. They are also attractive to companies with an unquantifiable exposure such as sales or expenses abroad that are difficult to predict precisely or with a balance sheet exposure created by foreign subsidiaries.

While the cases shown in Figures 19–22 explain the basic function of currency options, many variations and permutations have been developed by various banks and they are best suited to explain them in detail.

11 Financial Futures

Financial Futures were introduced into Britain from the Chicago Mercantile Exchange in 1982 and the London International Financial Futures Exchange (LIFFE) started trading in September of that year. Unlike the forward market where business is conducted by telephone or telex, financial futures are traded verbally in 'pits' on the floor of the exchange by brokers.

A financial futures contract is a binding agreement between a seller to deliver and a buyer to take up delivery of a specific currency at an agreed exchange rate or funds at an agreed interest rate, on a stated date. Although such a contract is binding between both parties, unlike a forward contract, in practice those commitments can be, and usually are, easily cancelled out by offsetting arrangements.

The financial futures market is very different from the forward market in so far that it follows the practice of the commodity market treating money as any other commodity. While the forward market will handle virtually any reasonable amount for any reasonable period, up to five years for most of the major currencies, financial futures contracts are standardised contracts for specified amounts with delivery on specified dates. For example the LIFFE Euro-dollar contract consists of one million US dollars for notional delivery on the third Wednesday of March, June, September and December each year.

The method of pricing financial futures is also very different from the forward market. The prices of short-term interest rate contracts are determined by an index calculated by subtracting from 100 the interest rate on the instrument involved. For example, a price of 87.50 implies an interest rate of 12.50 per cent.

Whereas the forward market will fix exchange rates for the sale

57

or purchase of currencies on or about a predetermined date in the future, financial futures will provide the corporate treasurer with the means of exercising his view of the future level of interest or exchange rates. As with currency options, however, many variations and permutations have been developed and those banks and institutions which specialise in this market are best suited to explain them in detail.

12   European Currency Units (ECUs)

The ECU is a basket of fixed amounts of EEC currencies, the composition of which is occasionally revised to allow in new member countries. It is closely linked to the EMS and was designed as an initial step in providing greater stability from fluctuating exchange rates. The exchange rates of those countries which have become full members of the EMS are fixed within a narrow band to an ECU central rate, whereas the exchange rates for those countries which are not full members of the EMS float against a theoretical or imputed ECU central rate. The exact weight of each currency as a percentage of the whole depends on its current exchange rate and changes continually. Table 5 shows the ECU central rates and corresponding percentage weights on 1 September 1989.

In its ten years existence, the ECU has grown very fast and its

Table 5

Currencies	ECU central rates (all=1 ECU)	Weights (%)
Deutschmark	2.05853	30.10
French franc	6.90403	19.00
Sterling	0.728627 (imputed rate)	13.00
Dutch guilder	2.31943	9.40
Belgian and Luxemburg francs	42.4582	7.90
Italian lira	1483.58	10.15
Danish krone	7.85212	2.45
Irish punt	0.768411	1.10
Greek drachma	150.792 (imputed rate)	0.80
Spanish peseta	133.804	5.30
Portugese escudo	172.085 (imputed rate)	0.80

use in European commercial transactions continues to increase and not only by the EEC countries. The USSR has recently announced for example, that for major consortium contracts in future it will consider ECUs in order to minimise exchange rate movements. It has also been reported that the airlines have also recently announced that instead of using the US dollar for reconciliation purposes, currently running at approximately $15 billion, they are considering the ECU. A growing number of companies and particularly those with wide European representation, are already dealing in ECUs. Moreover, by 1992 it is expected that Europe will have become a single trading entity and the establishment of European prices in ECUs will then become increasingly desirable in order to maintain a stable distribution network.

Table 6   Currency rates, 11 September 1989

	Bank rate (%)	Special drawing rights	European Currency Unit
Sterling	—	1.25154	1.47882
US dollar	7	1.23648	1.04239
Canadian dollar	12.36	1.46857	1.23742
Austrian Schilling	5	17.2613	14.6185
Belgian franc	7.75	51.2799	43.4415
Danish krone	9.50	9.52090	8.06652
Deutschmark	5.00	2.45219	2.07717
Dutch guilder	6.00	2.76415	2.34079
French franc	9.50	8.25969	6.99756
Italian lira	13.50	1757.59	1488.53
Japanese yen	3.25	181.268	153.721
Norwegian krone	8	8.91997	7.54794
Spanish peseta	—	152.951	129.517
Swedish krone	9.50	8.25721	6.98817
Swiss franc	5.50	2.11624	1.79426
Greek drachma	20.50	211.172	179.009
Irish punt	—	0.918560	0.778250

Sterling quoted in terms of SDR and ECU per £

So far as the trader is concerned, the ECU need only be seen as merely another currency whose spot rate is shown every day in the press. The figures shown in Table 6 are an extract from the *Financial Times*. They show a spot rate of ECU 1.47882 = £1, which is slightly different from the mean spot rate of ECU 1.47525 shown in the Day's Spread column of Table 3. All the other currencies shown in Table 6 are against the ECU, i.e. DM2.07717 = ECU 1.

Figure 23 assumes that a UK exporter wishes to establish an ECU price against a sterling price of £100,000 and a Deutschmark price of DM307,000. At a spot rate of £1 = ECU 1.47882, £100,000 = ECU 147,882. Deutschmarks 2.07717 = 1 ECU, therefore 147,882 ECUs = DM307,176.

Figure 23   European Currency Unit

£1 = ECUs 1.47882
∴ £100,000 = ECU 147,882

DM2.07717 = 1 ECU
∴ ECU 147,882 = DM307,176

Spot DM3.0700 = £1
∴ £100,000 = DM307,000

The spot rate for Deutschmarks is DM3.0700 = £1, therefore £100,000 equals DM307,000. There is only a margin of 176 Deutschmarks in the difference between the Deutschmark price and the ECU price. Even this is probably only a reflection of the different sources of the *Financial Times* figures.

While the ECU is basically devised as a stabilizing influence, there is nevertheless already a considerable and growing forward market in London for ECUs. This operates in exactly the same way as the forward market for any other currency and is based on the difference between the ECU deposit rates shown in Table 7, extracted from the *Financial Times*, and the Euro-currency interest rates.

Table 7   London money rates, 11 September 1989

	One month	Three months	Six months	One year
ECU-linked Deposit offer	9⁷⁄₁₆	9¾	9¾	9¹¹⁄₁₆
ECU-linked Deposit bid	9⁵⁄₁₆	9⅝	9⅝	9⁹⁄₁₆

Figures 24 and 25 show a UK export contract of £600,000 with payments at 1, 3, 6 and 12 months negotiated in French francs and lire. If the contract was negotiated in French francs and the

Figure 24   Exporting in ECUs

Spot FF10.0850 = £1

£600,000 = FF6,051,000 ÷ 4 = 1,512,750

1 month	10.0890 =	£149,940
3 months	10.0930 =	149,881
6 months	10.0690 =	150,238
12 months	10.0000 =	151,275

£601,334 = 0.22%

Figure 25   Exporting in ECUs

Spot Lira2232 = £1

£600,000 = Lire1339.2m ÷ 4 = 334,800,000

1 month	2243 =	£149,264	
3 months	2257 =	148,339	
6 months	2265 =	147,815	Discount
12 months	2290 =	146,201	£8381

£591,619 = 1.40%

four payments sold forward, the total premium involved would be £1334, i.e. an additional margin of 0.22 per cent on the face value of the contract. If the contract was negotiated in lire, and the payments sold forward, the discount involved would be £8381 or a loss of 1.40 per cent indicating that the lire price might have to be increased by 1.40 per cent.

If the contract shown in Figure 26 was negotiated in ECUs in either France or Italy and the payments sold forward, the total premium would be £6925, i.e. an increase of £5591 or 0.93 per cent over a French franc contract and an increase on £15,306 or 2.55 per cent over a lira contract. Armed with this knowledge a sales executive would be in a stronger negotiating position as he could, if pushed, reduce the ECU price by the amount of the premium.

Figure 26   Exporting in ECUs

Spot £0.6557 = ECU 1 ∴ £1 = ECU 1.5250

£600,000 = ECU 915,000 ÷ 4 = 228,750

1 month	1.5216 =	£150,335
3 months	1.5156 =	150,929
6 months	1.5049 =	152,004
12 months	1.4887 =	153,657

£606,925 = 1.15%

In the case shown in Figure 27 of an importer paying in Deutschmarks at six or twelve months and buying the currency forward, he would be obliged to pay premiums of £3332 or £6879 respectively. If he arranged to purchase in ECUs however, and bought them forward he would only pay premiums of £2171 and £4302.

Figure 27   Importing in ECUs

Spot ECU 1.47882 = £1	£100,000 = ECUs 147,882
6 months forward	1.44647 = £102,171
12 months forward	1.41782 = £104,302
Spot DM3.0700 = £1	£100,000 = DM307,000
6 months forward	2.9710 = £103,332
12 months forward	2.8724 = £106,879

---

13   Borrowing Currencies

Basically there are two kinds of borrowings in foreign currency. There is a borrowing of foreign currency in order to fund the sale of goods or services and there is a borrowing of foreign currency for investment purposes. With regard to borrowing foreign currency in order to fund the sale of goods there are basically two kinds of sale. There is the 'one-off' sale where the product is of considerable value and the 'on-going' sale of small units. There are in turn two types of borrowing to suit each type of sale. There is a term loan and an overdraft. Figure 28 shows a sale to Germany concluded in June 1989 and valued at 3.0375m Deutschmarks which will be payable in twelve months time. There are two ways in which this deal can be transacted and the exporter's risk eliminated. He can either fund the twelve months credit by borrowing

Figure 28

Currency Term Loan, 23 June 1989
UK base rate 14% – 12 months Euro-DM 7%
Spot DM3.0375 = £1
One sale of DM3.0375, single payment 12 months

Borrow DM3,037,500 for 12 months at a margin over 7% fixed
and convert at DM3.0375 = £1 providing £1m
DM receivables will go to repay the loan

If used for series of sales total has to be collected
over 12 months and repaid in one

Note: Borrowing rate for currency should normally be geared to
same level above interbank rate as above base

---

sterling and sell the Deutschmarks forward at a premium, which of course is based on the difference in the Euro-currency interest rates.

As an alternative however, he could borrow 3,037,500 Euro-Deutschmarks for a term of twelve months at a margin over 7 per cent per annum fixed. On day 1 the bank would give him the Deutschmarks which he would convert into sterling at the spot rate, thus yielding £1m. His liability to the bank, however, remains in Deutschmarks, but if he is going to receive Deutschmarks at the end of twelve months then these will merely be used when they come in to pay off the debt and the exporter does not have an exchange risk. On his balance sheet he will have an asset by way of a receivable of Deutschmarks 3.0375m and on the other side of the balance sheet he will have a liability by way of a borrowing of Deutschmarks 3.0375m. As the forward premium is calculated on the difference in the Euro-currency interest rates in the first place, there is no difference basically in the cost of selling the Deutschmarks forward or borrowing the Deutschmarks at the lower interest rate. It may, however, be administratively more convenient for the exporter to borrow the currency as opposed to selling forward. Should the payment be delayed beyond the 12 months the loan could either be extended for a further fixed term albeit shorter than 12 months if necessary, and at a different rate of interest, or it could be changed from a term basis to an overdraft as described in the following paragraphs. Should the overseas buyer fail to pay, then the exporter would have to buy the currency at the spot rate and could win or lose depending on the movement of the spot rate since conversion from sterling into currency. If he insures with ECGD, however, and incurs a loss covered by his policy, the additional loss which he may suffer by having to buy the currency may also be covered.

If the exporter is selling on an on-going basis and therefore never knows when orders are going to come in and for how much, he may choose to fund these sales by way of a Euro-currency overdraft.

Figure 29 shows a case based on a conservative estimate of the exporter's budgeted sales for 12 months of £1m. He arranges an overdraft in Euro-Deutschmarks and converts it all at the spot rate, i.e. DM3.0375 = £1. Henceforth all quotes and prices, including price lists, are geared to that one rate until the total facility is committed. As Deutschmark payments are received they merely go to reduce the overdraft until it is extinguished and the exporter has no exchange risk. While the overdraft renders the exporter vulnerable to changes in the interest rate in the same way as he is with his sterling overdraft, nevertheless in 1989 the cost of a DM overdraft on average would have been a margin over an average rate of 7.06 per cent per annum compared with the average UK base rate of 13.85 per cent per annum.

Figure 29

Currency Overdraft, 23 June 1989
UK base rate 14% p.a. – Euro-DM 6⅜% p.a.
12 months: budgeted sales to Germany £1m

Borrow DM3,037,500 and convert at spot DM3.0375 = £1
Providing £1m on which interest will fluctuate day to day

Quotes and sales all converted at
DM 3.0375 until total facility committed
Convert next £1m at new rate

If spot rate not good enough to go forward
12 months at a time take 6 or 3 months budgeted sales.

The advantage of the currency overdraft is the flexibility which it provides. If the budgeted sales are exceeded the overdraft will last a shorter period at the initial conversion rate; if sales have been over-estimated the overdraft will last longer at the initial conversion rate. If the spot rate of exchange goes substantially in the exporter's favour during the course of the initial conversion, he can take any particular transaction outside the scope of the overdraft and use the forward market thus obtaining the benefit of the better rate. This will merely have the effect of extending the overdraft over a longer period.

Figure 30 shows the average 90-day Euro-currency borrowing rates in 1989 for the six major currencies. These will give the reader a very good idea of the advantages which arise from selling in local currencies as opposed to sterling.

Figure 30   Average 90-day Euro-currency borrowing rates, 1989.

Euro-currencies	
Deutschmark	7.06% p.a.
Guilder	7.33% p.a.
Swiss franc	7.06% p.a.
Yen	5.42% p.a.
Sterling	13.87% p.a.
US dollar	9.26% p.a.

Reverting to borrowing currencies for investment purposes, this may have little relation to trade and is conducted purely as part of the overall treasury function. It is nevertheless important to guard against the exchange risk whenever possible.

14   Offsetting Imports with Exports

Where a company or group has transactions of exports say in guilders and imports payable also in guilders, it is quite often tempting to try and balance receivables with payables, thus assuming there is no exchange risk. This practice can be very dangerous. It is not so much a question of balancing the imports with the exports but the cash flow that matters. If a company has got to pay guilders today or within the next few days but is not expecting to receive guilders for another three months, then it will merely have to buy the guilders at the spot rate of exchange and of course it has thus incurred the whole of the exchange risk. So, any function which tries to balance exports with imports in the same currency should primarily look at the cash flow position. Nevertheless, having said this, such a company is not getting the best possible result from its transactions.

If a company which is exporting and importing in a currency which is at a premium against sterling, such as the Dutch guilder, and is using its receivables in order to pay for its imports, then of course it cannot sell the currency forward and earn the premium nor borrow against it at a lower interest rate. The salesman, however, may require to use that additional margin in order to reduce the price and make himself more competitive. This of course is now denied to him, and he may even lose the business. In order to get the best of both worlds therefore and without running exchange risks, the company should be selling in guilders and earning the premium but its buyers should negotiate their purchases from Holland at fixed sterling prices as close to the spot rate as possible thereby reducing the cost of the purchase by the amount of the premium.

Many buyers seem to think that such a negotiated purchase price is impossible but this may well stem from the fact that few

understand how to negotiate in currencies and merely refer it all
to 'finance'. Unfortunately, by the time it gets to 'finance' it is
usually too late. Many buyers, including some who spend large
sums overseas, hide behind the fear that if they argue about
currency their suppliers will refuse to supply them. It is difficult
to imagine any exporter wantonly turning away good business
from an important client simply because the buyer wants to pay
in his own currency.

Part II
Applying the Technology to Export and Import Transactions

15 Marketing and Sales

In 1981 there appeared in the *Guardian* newspaper a half-page article proclaiming in its headline that in the previous year Britain lost £800 million through foreign exchange ignorance. This was not a reflection on the banks' foreign exchange dealers but on the inability of our exporters and importers to grasp this particular nettle and by making use of the facilities which the banks provide generate more profit, obtain better market penetration by improving their competitiveness and cut costs on their imports.

By 1989 the overall situation was even worse. While surveys indicate that exports invoiced in local currencies to the EEC countries may have risen to approximately 45 per cent and those to North America to 55 per cent, the total of additional benefits which Britain's exporters and importers denied themselves was in the region of £1.4 billion.

From a marketing point of view and because of the fierce competition in world markets we must continually be striving to make it easier for buyers to buy our products as opposed to someone else's, and certainly one way in which this can be achieved is to sell to the buyer in his own currency or in a currency to which his is more closely allied, i.e. the US dollar. Those developing countries which are dependent on World Bank or IMF loans are more likely to wish to pay in US dollars. Moreover, approximately 60 per cent of the world's trade is now conducted in dollars.

In order to underline this need of marketing overseas in foreign currencies one only has to look back to the mid-1970s in order to appreciate the extent to which we got it wrong at that time. Because approximately 90 per cent of all our exports were being invoiced in sterling and because of inflation within the

UK, we were continually having to increase the sterling price. If you take a three-year period in the mid-1970s for example, we were having to increase our sterling prices by at least 1–1½ per cent every month simply because of inflation at home.

If you ask any buyer what he looks for more than anything else from a supplier he will invariably tell you, 'at least stable prices for a reasonable period and reductions if possible', and that is precisely what we could not give our overseas buyers at that time. As a result of that one fact we lost a very large slice of our overseas mass markets.

If we had been selling to Denmark and invoicing our sales to Denmark in Danish kroner during that same three-year period, we could have reduced our Danish kroner prices by approximately 30 per cent. If we had been selling to Germany and invoicing our sales to Germany in Deutschmarks we could have reduced our Deutschmark prices by over 90 per cent in that three-year period, instead of which we were selling in sterling, increasing our sterling prices every month and losing the market. And this is not the benefit of hindsight. These facts and figures were known and were available at the time but unfortunately the technology of foreign exchange was even less understood then than it is today.

'Oh, the risk!' is the cry that often goes up from British exporters when it is suggested to them that they might be better-off selling overseas in foreign currencies. 'If I invoice my buyer for sterling £10,000 then I know I am going to receive sterling £10,000 and all the risk of fluctuating exchange rates has gone away.' No part of any risk has gone away because the exporter has invoiced his buyer in sterling. All that he has done is transferred the risk to his buyer who will not have anything like the facilities available to him as we have in London with which to protect himself. Well, that may be all right if the exporter is in a seller's market and can afford to adopt that attitude but very few sellers are in that position today. Everyone is virtually in a buyer's market and we should continually remind ourselves of that fact. Any UK importer being offered a fixed competitive price in sterling as opposed to a foreign currency would confirm the attractiveness of such a deal, provided of course that it was also the 'correct' sterling price.

As has already been shown, it is particularly important for those exporters selling to distributors overseas to be selling in local currency. If they are selling in sterling and passing on the exchange risk to the distributor, leaving him to fix the local currency price, he will invariably load it by a substantial margin to protect his profit. Consequently that product may well be sold at much too high a price and certainly it will be less competitive than it need be.

Moreover, a sale in sterling may very well be seen by the overseas distributor as an invitation to him to gamble on the exchange rate at the exporter's expense. If the rate goes in his favour he will most certainly not offer to pay a proportion of his gain to the exporter but if it goes against him he may very well ask the exporter to make up part of the loss. Indeed, many exporters who do not understand the technology of foreign exchange enter into the most convoluted arrangements with their overseas distributors in order to try and even out such gains and losses whereas they could so easily offer their distributors fixed local currency prices, even at a reduction, and with no exchange risk.

If the spot rate of exchange at the time the deal with the distributor is struck is not particularly attractive then the exporter need only cover the projected sales over a shorter period, say 3 or 6 months as opposed to 12 months. This may entail a local price adjustment at say 3 or 6 months but if it is downwards it will do no harm and if it is upwards the forward premium or the lower interest rate at which the exporter is funding the sale may be able to absorb the increase.

Exporters selling to distributors in those countries whose exchange rates tend to be more volatile than say the Deutschmark, yen or Swiss franc are often rather more fearful to sell in local currencies particularly if the currency concerned is at a discount against sterling. It should be remembered, however, that it is in fact the distributors in such countries who, when establishing their local currency prices, will tend to load their prices by a much higher margin in order to offset the more volatile movements in the exchange rate and thus make the British product even less competitive. It is even more important therefore in these countries to be selling in local currencies as more often than not the discount on the forward sale or the additional cost of borrowing the Euro-currency involved is much less than the additional margin with which the distributor will load his price if asked to absorb the exchange risk.

While it is generally agreed that the large majority of British exporters and importers, particularly at operational levels, have relatively little knowledge of how the foreign exchange market works in the UK and how best to apply the various techniques to commercial transactions, it is nevertheless assumed that all our overseas buyers and suppliers are somehow endowed with all the knowledge about foreign exchange which we do not possess. There is absolutely no evidence to support such an assumption. Indeed, quite the reverse is the case. All the evidence points to the fact that with very few exceptions they understand it even less than we do. The one country in which a British exporter or importer is most likely to meet a buyer or supplier who understands the forward market is Holland.

More often than not, however, overseas buyers and suppliers are good actors in so far that they give the impression of wheeling and dealing in foreign exchange and nod-nod-wink-wink know all about it. The best way to call the bluff of an overseas buyer or supplier in such circumstances is to ask what forward rate his bank quoted him that morning or could you use his phone to find out. He will then usually begin to prevaricate and say he never uses the forward market because of course that is gambling and he never gambles. If he is that very rare bird, however, that does understand the forward market then no British export or import executive should ever be in the position of not knowing as much about it as his opposite number. He must always be negotiating at least on level terms.

A good example of a major overseas buyer who did not understand the forward market, at least at operational level, is illustrated in the following case study:

A British engineering company had been asked by a major buyer in Germany to quote for a £3m contract. They also stipulated that they wished the quote to be in sterling. This fact prompted the impression that they might well be gambling on the devaluation of sterling against the Deutschmark in which event the sterling would cost them fewer Deutschmarks when they came to pay.

Having prepared his sterling quotation the exporter decided to submit a Deutschmark quotation as well. Should the buyer decide on the Deutschmark quotation the premium on the forward sale of the Deutschmarks would represent an additional margin of approximately 15 per cent on the face value of the contract. This would not only provide him with a very substantial cushion against any exchange risk during the three months quotation period, but also allow him to reduce the Deutschmark price by 7 per cent.

On receipt of the two quotations the buyer converted the sterling quotation into Deutschmarks at the spot rate and discovered that the Deutschmark price was considerably cheaper than the sterling price and sent a telex asking the exporter to confirm the two quotations as he thought that there had been a mistake, particularly because the UK exporter was now level pegging with a local German supplier. On receipt of the confirmation he accepted the Deutschmark quotation against the local competition.

In some countries they have no forward market at all and in others only very limited facilities. Any UK exporter selling to them in sterling, therefore, is indeed making it very difficult for the buyer to buy his product simply because he may not be able to protect himself against the exchange risk even if he knew how. On the other hand if we convert our prices into their currency we can give them the benefit of the London money market. We are not therefore asking our overseas buyers to do *us* a favour by paying us in foreign currencies, we are doing *them* a favour.

The speed at which Glasnost and Perestroika has precipitated change in the USSR itself but even more particularly in the East European countries makes it difficult to assess the final outcome. There is no doubt however, that all these countries will require and will be seeking economic help on a huge scale from the western democracies and that this will present great opportunities to our exporters. This help is bound to be denominated in various currencies including the ECU and British exporters must therefore be ready and willing to deal in any of these currencies. A British exporter expecting to sell only in sterling will be presenting a very narrow catchment area and it will be essential that he let it be known that he is very happy to accept payment in any of the major currencies. After all, provided there is a forward market for the currency he has nothing to fear and may even be able to make more profit or offer a more competitive price. In any event he will be providing a very much wider catchment area to the East European countries.

In addition to making it easier for the buyer to pay in his own currency, the biggest possible incentive for British exporters to sell in foreign currencies as opposed to sterling is reflected in the fact that in 179 currency years out of 242, British exporters could have sold currencies forward at a premium. This means that they could have earned more profit or been able to make themselves more competitive. Table 2 (p.79) shows the amounts available over the years 1987–1989.

Bearing in mind that premiums/discounts are merely a reflection of the difference in Euro-currency interest rates, the statistics show that in 179 currency years out of 242, UK interest rates were higher than our competitors. This means that at the time of writing, against a UK base rate of 14 per cent per annum, our German competitors for example, were only paying approximately 8 per cent per annum for their money. In those terms it is not difficult to understand why they have been so successful. By invoicing in Deutschmarks however, and either earning the premium by selling them forward or funding the sale by way of a borrowing of Euro-Deutschmarks at approximately 8 per cent per annum, we can bring ourselves down to their level of cost of money.

How often in the past have we heard the cry that with such high interest rates 'we can't compete in export markets!' In those circumstances the real answer must surely be 'don't sell in sterling. Sell in the other country's currency and plug yourself into the lower interest rate'. If you are fully competitive when selling in sterling then you have made up the difference in the interest rates and you are extremely competitive and fully deserve to keep the extra profit.

As in everything else, however, an approach to an overseas buyer to pay in a different currency to that in which he is used to paying, has to be made with conviction. It has to be 'sold', particularly if that buyer does not understand the technology of foreign exchange and is merely used to taking a view on what he thinks the spot rate is likely to be at some future date. It is essential therefore that sales executives should at least be able to explain it to overseas buyers with skill and conviction.

Table 2 (see also p.26.)

	1987 (£)	1988 (£)	1989 (£)	Totals (£)
US dollar	6 075	5 625	10 875	22 575
Canadian dollar	2 825	1 525	4 000	8 350
Netherlands guilder	10 600	13 475	15 450	39 525
Belgian franc	6 250	8 625	12 575	27 450
Deutschmark	13 850	14 575	16 200	44 625
French franc	2 350	5 000	10 750	18 100
Austrian schilling	12 100	13 100	15 200	40 400
Swiss franc	14 350	17 550	16 375	48 275
Japanese yen	13 375	14 000	20 350	47 725
Totals	81 775	93 475	121 775	297 025

16   'I've Got a Contract'

This is a statement which is heard very often but which is not often exactly true. The salesman may consider that the arrangement he has with his buyer constitutes a contract, whereas it may only state the buyer's intention, albeit his hopeful intention. If it is relied on, however, and the currency sold forward it could lead to an embarrassing situation if the buyer's hopes are not fulfilled. This kind of situation highlights the need to apply the basic disciplines which may best be illustrated by using the simile of electricity. If misused or mishandled an electric circuit hopefully will only blow a fuse. It could, however, cause a fire or even worse, an explosion. With this knowledge we have come to know that there must be a disciplined approach to matters electric. In exactly the same way, matters of foreign exchange require a disciplined approach in order to avoid embarrassment, let alone fire or explosion.

A 'contract' which is not a firm commitment but merely a hopeful intention can cause problems when dealing with the foreign exchange aspect. Sales executives should therefore be careful to differentiate between the two and ensure that good commercial discipline is always applied. The advantages of selling overseas in currency are such that mere expediency should not be allowed to justify sales in sterling. Moreover, the advantages are such that exports in currency should be negotiated in the best possible way and with the greatest possible care.

17   Quoting

Quoting in foreign currencies can give rise to exchange risks and care must therefore be taken to minimise or remove the risk altogether. There are several ways in which this can be achieved:

1. Those exporters who have traditionally always sold in sterling can continue to quote and/or even publish price-lists in sterling but with the proviso that the sterling prices will be converted into the appropriate currency at the spot rate ruling in London on receipt of a firm order. This is tantamount to saying to the buyer that he will take the exchange risk up to the time he has decided to give the exporter an order but on doing so the exporter will then take the risk right up to the time when the buyer is due to pay. This is still an infinitely better deal than saying to the buyer that he must take the whole of the risk for the full period.

2. Quote in currency but subject to a validity period which should be kept as short as possible and subject to a currency clause drafted by solicitors along the following lines:

    This quotation is calculated at an exchange rate of $x = £1$, but if the rate moves more than y per cent [whatever tolerance the exporter can carry and perhaps include in his price] during the validity period of this quotation, then *either* party reserves the right to re-negotiate the price.

    If the exporter can be seen to be protecting the interests of the buyer as well as his own, the buyer is not likely to object. If the clause only takes care of the exporter's interest, the buyer may well object to the clause and insist on its removal leaving the exporter fully exposed to the exchange risk.

3. In the case of on-going sales on short terms of credit, the

problem of quoting or publishing price-lists in currencies may best be overcome by either selling forward an amount of currency based on a conservative estimate of the budgeted sales over a given period, say 12 months or by arranging an overdraft facility in the currency concerned for a similar amount and converting it at the current spot rate. Thereafter the one rate of exchange in each case will govern all quotations, price-lists and sales until the forward contract or drawdown has been fully committed.

4.   As will be seen in the following case studies, the premiums involved and particularly in some long-term contracts, can be very substantial, i.e. up to and over 15 per cent flat on the face value of the contract. In these circumstances, the premium may well be sufficient or even more than adequate to offset any adverse movement in the exchange rate during the validity period of the quotation.

5.   A currency option may provide the necessary protection provided that the cost involved can be absorbed into the contract or by the premium which would accrue on the forward sale of the currency should the quote be successful.

6.   The ECGD's 'Tender to Contract' cover may also be used.

18   Pricing

An additional margin of say 8 per cent per annum or 2 per cent flat on goods being sold into Japan on an on-going basis with an average period of three months between date of order and date of payment, must surely be taken into one's overall strategy. It cannot be left as 'financial perks', because part of the marketing strategy might well require a reduction in price of 2 per cent, the failure of which might mean loss of orders. For the same reason the receivables concerned cannot be merely hived off to pay for imports, otherwise the 2 per cent is no longer available as the means of providing the reduction in price.

In the case of capital goods sold on extended terms of credit, the additional margins available from the forward sale of certain currencies can be very substantial indeed ranging up to 21 per cent on the face value of the contract. In cases such as these it is essential that the currency aspect be taken into account not only from a pricing viewpoint but also with regard to quoting and the competition with which the exporter may be confronted.

With regard to imports direct from overseas payable in currencies, the buyer has to calculate the price of buying the currency forward in order to evaluate the whole cost of the import. Confronted by a sterling price offered to him by an overseas supplier, the buyer must be able to calculate the 'correct' sterling price as opposed to what may merely appear to be a 'good' sterling price.

When buying imported goods in sterling from a UK importing agent the buyer must be careful to avoid an inflated sterling price into which the importing agent has loaded a bigger margin than the forward premium in order to protect himself against the exchange risk.

19 Purchasing

In 1980 a survey was conducted on purchasing methods as part of manufacturing industry's drive to cut costs and the surveyors noted the disproportionate increase in company profits which can result from improvements in purchasing tactics. Their findings showed that a 2 per cent reduction in the cost of purchases could yield a 10 per cent addition to profit. They also claimed that a 5 per cent reduction in material costs would have an equivalent effect on profitability as a 10 per cent increase in sales.

These figures should be well borne in mind when the reader studies the cases shown on the following pages of the book and might do well to assess the additional profits which would have accrued to the companies concerned by virtue of the savings in cost. Moreover, he might do even better by assessing the situation in his own company.

Although the purchase of material and components typically accounts for approximately 60 per cent of sales revenue in manufacturing industry, the departments involved have traditionally carried less status within companies compared with say production or marketing. It is not unknown for example, for the purchasing department to consist of a few clerks who merely enact the instructions of the engineers and in these circumstances it is not difficult to imagine how a certain company came to pay 17½ per cent too much for its machine tool by buying it from Switzerland instead of France.

Most senior buying executives would rightly claim to be expert at selecting the best product at the best price. When dealing across frontiers, however, it is essential to take account of the built-in price of the currency involved. It is not sufficient merely to look at the spot rate of exchange and consider the value in sterling terms converted at that rate unless of course payment is going to be made at that time. If payment is to be made at some time in the future, then appropriate calculations have to be made to ascertain the cost at the forward rate of exchange. If the currency is at a discount then it is in order to pay in that currency because the discount will reduce the cost of the product. If the currency is at a premium which will increase the cost of the product, then the buyer must know this so that he can offset as much of the premium as possible in his negotiations. In today's buyer's market no self-respecting buyer should expect to have to pay a substantial amount over and above the cost of the product for the doubtful privilege of paying the supplier in his own currency.

The most favourable deal for the buyer is to offer a fixed sterling price converted at the current spot rate, or as close to it as possible, but payable at the future date. If this offer is made at the time when the buyer is about to place a firm order it very often succeeds. If the buyer suspects, or at worst has assumed that his supplier knows more about the forward market than he does, he should stop and ask himself on what grounds he has based his assumption. The facts, backed by firm evidence, show that very few overseas suppliers ever use the forward market, let alone know anything about it. In many countries there is no forward market, in many others, even leading industrial countries, the forward market is so undeveloped that very few people use it. If the supplier is so knowledgeable and there is a forward market in his country, then he can just as easily sell to his UK buyer in sterling but would merely have to load the sterling price by the amount of the discount he is going to lose on the forward sale of sterling.

A major British company intent on placing a large contract with an overseas supplier obtained his quotation in currency. After a good deal of negotiations both agreed a currency price. Before placing the order, however, the British importer requested a quotation in sterling mainly in order to ascertain if the supplier understood the forward market. The subsequent quotation in sterling was completely outwith and bore no relation either to the spot rate or the forward rate but merely indicated that the supplier was not conversant with the forward market and consequently was loading the sterling price by a very large amount in order to offset the exchange risk. With this in mind the buyer made sterling offers at various levels in excess of the spot rate but well below the ceiling of the forward rate. The final fixed sterling price which was agreed involved a premium of only £85,000 as opposed to the premium calculated at the forward rate of £200,000.

Before a buyer agrees an initial sterling price either direct from an overseas supplier or from a UK importing agent, he should seek to know the currency price as he will otherwise be unable to calculate the exchange rate at which the sterling price has been converted and compare this rate with the spot and forward rates. This may not always be easy but the buyer is at a very substantial disadvantage if he has to accept what merely appears to be a good sterling price.

As an alternative to offering a fixed sterling price based on the current spot rate, the buyer could offer a fixed sterling price based on a rate halfway between the spot and forward rates. He could then explain that they were each carrying half the cost of the currency. In any event and whatever the outcome, by understanding the technology and knowing how to apply it, the UK buyer has placed himself in the strongest possible negotiating position. He knows the facts and does not have to rely on guesswork or even worse, waffle.

Where the buyer is considering a purchase from a country whose currency is at a premium against sterling, that premium indicates that the supplier's cost of money is lower than that in the UK. In these circumstances and provided the deal has been struck in sterling, the buyer should not stifle his temptation to extract the maximum credit. Depending on his own company's cash position, he might even offer to pay for such credit at an interest rate slightly higher than that which the supplier is paying but lower than that which his own company is paying.

Some buying executives tend to hide their lack of knowledge and understanding of this technology by stating that unless they pay in the supplier's currency, the supplier will refuse to supply them. This has even been said by buyers responsible for purchases valued at many millions of pounds annually and can only be taken as a poor excuse. What exporter anywhere in the world with that kind of volume would turn business away simply because the buyer wanted to negotiate a price in his own currency as opposed to that of the supplier?

If the overseas supplier insists on payment in his own currency as opposed to sterling and if that currency is at a premium, the UK buyer should equally insist on a penalty clause for delay or non-delivery. Having bought the currency forward he may be obliged to extend or even close out his forward contract and if the rate has gone against him this may cost him money.

The purchase of imported goods from UK agents needs to be looked at closely. In many cases the importing agent does not use the forward market in order to cover his exchange risk with the overseas supplier and protects himself by loading the sterling price. This loading is invariably much higher than the cost of buying the currency forward and the UK buyer is therefore paying too high a price. A typical example is a UK agent buying from Italy and loading the sterling selling price by as much as 20 per cent to protect himself against the exchange risk. At the time he could have bought lire forward at a discount. Any buyer purchasing from UK import agents needs to understand the technology so as to ensure that he is not paying what appears to be a good price but which in fact is more expensive than it needs to be.

20 Case Studies

Exports

Figure 31 provides an excellent example of how the forward market works in a commercial way. A British chemical manufacturer had quoted a price of $772 per ton to a Malaysian buyer for a type of fertiliser. Two weeks later one of the company's salesmen was in Malaysia in the hope of closing the sale. He was told, however, that a competitor was quoting a price of $704 per ton, a reduction of 8.8 per cent and so he rang his head office to enquire if he could meet it. If they were to get the order it would entail three shipments and consequently three payments at 6, 8 and 10 months. At the current spot rate the contract would produce a price of £449 per ton and their minimum price was £420 per ton. They enquired from their bank what the forward rates would be for delivery of dollars at the required intervals of 6, 8 and 10 months at the reduced price of $704 and were given rates which would produce £422, £426 and £432 per ton respectively.

In a matter of a few minutes they could advise the sales

Figure 31

UK Exporter quoted US $772 per ton
Spot rate $1.7170 = £1
@ 1.7170 $772 = £449 min. price £420
? $704 per ton

Deliveries: SEPT–NOV–JAN
Forward rates 1.6670–1.6510–1.6300
$704 = £422–£426–£432

---

executive in the field and enable him to requote the price to meet the competition. Without the use of the forward market, however, and with all the imponderables involved they would have been hard-pressed to know whether they could meet the competition.

Figure 32 shows the details of a £5m contract negotiated in US dollars in February 1988 with payments spread at six-monthly intervals over five years. Against a conversion rate of $1.7735 = £1, the forward rates range from $1.7528 down to $1.6885 and yield in total a premium of £199,916 or an additional margin of 4 per cent.

Figure 32

---

26 February 1988 spot $1.7735 = £1
£5m = $8,867,500 ÷ 10 = $886,750

6 months	1.7528 = £505,905
12 months	1.7340 = 511,390
18 months	1.7185 = 516,002
24 months	1.7045 = 520,241
30 months	1.6985 = 522,078
36 months	1.6935 = 523,620
42 months	1.6885 = 525,170
48 months	1.6885 = 525,170
54 months	1.6885 = 525,170
60 months	1.6885 = 525,170

Total premium £199,916 = 4%

This additional margin merely reflects the differences in the interest rates between borrowings of 886, 750 Euro-dollars for each of the ten six-monthly payments on the day on which they were all sold forward, against ten corresponding loans of Euro-sterling.

While the additional profit may be of some value in obtaining the order, it would hardly be sufficient to act as a cushion against the adverse movement of the spot rate during the quotation period.

Compared with Figure 33 showing details of a similar contract in August 1987, it is interesting to note that whereas there had been a considerable movement in the spot rate from $1.5883 = £1 in August 1987 to $1.7735 = £1 in February 1988, the difference between the interest rates hardly moved and as a result the premium as a percentage of the value of the contracts remained virtually the same.

Figure 33

---

4 August 1987 spot $1.5883 = £1
£1m = $1,588,300 ÷ 10 = $158,830

6 months	1.5703 =	£101,146
12 months	1.5544 =	102,181
18 months	1.5415 =	103,036
24 months	1.5286 =	103,906
30 months	1.5227 =	104,308
36 months	1.5167 =	104,721
42 months	1.5128 =	104,991
48 months	1.5088 =	105,269
54 months	1.5039 =	105,612
60 months	1.4989 =	105,964

Total premium £41,134 = 4.11%

Figure 34 shows that in July 1989 the interest rate differential had doubled owing to the rising rates in Britain providing a premium of 8.77 per cent.

Figure 35 illustrates a £5m contract denominated in yen with payments at six-monthly intervals over five years and shows an additional margin by way of forward premium, of 12.81 per cent on the face value of the contract. This sum is surely sufficiently significant to alert any sales executive who is meeting Japanese competition say in Saudi Arabia to switch out of sterling into yen and thereby reduce his yen price to meet or even undercut the competition.

Figure 34

---

11 July 1989 spot $1.6245 = £1
£1m = $1,624,500 ÷ 10 = $162,450

6 months	1.5879 =	£102,305
12 months	1.5513 =	104,719
18 months	1.5274 =	106,357
24 months	1.5035 =	108,048
30 months	1.4902 =	109,009
36 months	1.4770 =	109,986
42 months	1.4670 =	110,736
48 months	1.4570 =	111,496
54 months	1.4482 =	112,170
60 months	1.4395 =	112,852

Total premium £87,678 = 8.77%

Figure 35

---

26 February 1988 spot yen 227.5 = £1
£5m = yen 1,137.5m ÷ 10 = 113,750,000

6 months	221.95 =	£512,503
12 months	215.95 =	526,742
18 months	212.25 =	535,925
24 months	208.25 =	546,218
30 months	204.25 =	556,916
36 months	200.25 =	568,040
42 months	196.25 =	579,618
48 months	192.25 =	591,678
54 months	188.15 =	604,571
60 months	184.00 =	618,207

Total premium £640,418 = 12.81%

Figure 36 shows that a similar contract in yen negotiated in July 1989 yielded a premium of 17.86 per cent. While the spot rate did not move, by virtue of the rising interest rates in Britain the premium increased by 39 per cent.

Figure 36

---

11 July 1989 spot yen 227.00 = £1
£1m = yen 227m ÷ 10 = 22,700,000

6 months	218.725 =	£103,783
12 months	210.45 =	107,864
18 months	204.725 =	110,880
24 months	199.000 =	114,040
30 months	194.500 =	116,710
36 months	190.000 =	119,474
42 months	186.000 =	122,043
48 months	182.000 =	124,725
54 months	177.500 =	127,887
60 months	173.000 =	131,214

Total premium £178,620 = 17.86%

Figure 37 gives details of a £4m contract which a British construction company obtained in Egypt in 1985. Again, the payments were at regular intervals over five years. The company had quoted in sterling but during the course of the negotiations they were informed that a German competitor had undercut them by 6 per cent. The company could not reduce its sterling price by anything like 6 per cent and therefore switched out of sterling into Deutschmarks and, as shown in Figure 37, were able to obtain a premium on the forward sale of the Deutschmarks of no less than 14.98 per cent on the value of the contract. In those circumstances they had no difficulty in reducing their Deutschmark price by 6 per cent and were subsequently awarded the contract.

Figure 38 shows that in February 1988 a similar contract in

Figure 37

---

13 September 1985 £4m @ spot dm3.8900 = £1
£4m = DM15,560,000 ÷ 10 DM1,556,000

6 months	3.7650 =	£413,280
12 months	3.6625 =	424,846
18 months	3.5750 =	435,245
24 months	3.4900 =	445,845
30 months	3.4150 =	455,637
36 months	3.3450 =	465,172
42 months	3.2750 =	475,115
48 months	3.2100 =	484,735
54 months	3.1450 =	494,754
60 months	3.0850 =	504,376

Total £4,599,005 = 14.98%

Figure 38

---

26 February 1988 spot DM2.9955 = £1
£5m = DM14,977,500 ÷ 10 = 1,497,750

6 months	2.9117 =	£514,390
12 months	2.8295 =	529,334
18 months	2.7630 =	542,074
24 months	2.6955 =	555,648
30 months	2.6505 =	565,082
36 months	2.6030 =	575,394
42 months	2.5755 =	581,538
48 months	2.5405 =	589,549
54 months	2.5105 =	596,594
60 months	2.4805 =	603,810

Total premium £653,413 = 13.07%

Deutschmarks yielded a premium of 13.07 per cent. It is worth noting in this case that while the spot rate between September 1985 and February 1988 moved no less than 90 pfennigs, the premium only moved 12.75 per cent because the interest rates were relatively stable.

Figure 39 shows a similar contract negotiated in May 1989 which again owing to the rising interest rates in the UK yielded an additional margin by way of forward premium of 17.8 per cent.

Figure 39

---

12 May 1989 spot DM3.1988 = £1
£5m = DM15,994,000 ÷ 10 = 1,599,400

6 months	3.0988 =	£516,135
12 months	2.9950 =	534,023
18 months	2.9175 =	548,209
24 months	2.8400 =	563,169
30 months	2.7650 =	578,445
36 months	2.6900 =	594,572
42 months	2.6150 =	611,625
48 months	2.5400 =	629,685
54 months	2.4650 =	648,844
60 months	2.3900 =	669,205

Total premium £893,912 = 17.8%

In Figure 40 a contract with ten equal payments over five years negotiated in Swiss francs in December 1986 yielded a premium of no less than 21.7 per cent.

It is difficult to imagine that any export executive going overseas either to negotiate a sale in Switzerland or having to combat Swiss competition in a third country should have such an additional margin with which to compete if necessary but does not know it is there.

When one ponders on the extent that we seem to exist at

Figure 40

---

3 December 1986 £4m @ spot SF2.3620 = £1
£4m = SF9,448,000 ÷ 10 = 944,800

6 months	2.3246 =	£406,436
12 months	2.2034 =	428,792
18 months	2.1212 =	445,408
24 months	2.0438 =	462,276
30 months	1.9702 =	479,545
36 months	1.8978 =	497,840
42 months	1.8435 =	512,503
48 months	1.7899 =	527,851
54 months	1.7342 =	544,805
60 months	1.6793 =	562,615

Total premium £868,071 = 21.70%

---

economic crisis level and yet have an entirely homespun technology which can so easily produce additional profit margins or increased competitiveness purely at the cost of a telephone call, one has to question the effectiveness of our training facilities. It is a known fact that as a nation we spend less on management training than any of our major competitors and this example must surely bring home the need to rectify that situation. Where else in any company could one phone call produce a reduction in cost, increased profit or competitiveness of 21.7 per cent?

Bearing in mind that premiums are merely a reflection of the difference in interest rates, there are an equal number of companies manufacturing small units and funding their exports by way of Euro-currency overdrafts. One such claims that in the first six months of switching his sales to Germany from sterling to Deutschmarks he reduced his cost of borrowing by over £100,000. Another is now funding his sales to his six overseas distributing subsidiaries by way of six Euro-currency overdrafts and expects to cut his cost of borrowing by at least £200,000 in the current twelve months.

In neither case has the company concerned had to employ a single extra member of staff. What little additional administration is involved has easily been absorbed by existing staff. In the case of the company running six currency overdrafts, this is managed by one financial accountant helped by a monitor updating the exchange and interest rates.

The burden of additional staff and a high increase in costs is often given as the reason for staying in sterling. This is an entirely false assumption. Experience shows that existing staff, properly trained and enthusiastic, can quite easily absorb the work involved.

Imports

Figure 41 illustrates an almost classic situation where no account was taken of the cost of buying the currency of the country from which the imported product was purchased.

Figure 41

Import order £100,000

Spot		12 months		
FF10.195	= £1	11.393	= £1	£89,486 − 10.51%
SwF3.10	= £1	2.898	= £1	£106,952 + 6.95%

The buyer in this case had two suppliers, one in France and one in Switzerland. He obtained quotations from each and they both quoted in their own currencies. On converting the quotations into sterling at the spot rate of exchange in order to evaluate them, the buyer found that they were very competitive with each other in sterling terms. As there was very little between the two prices he committed himself to the Swiss supplier and then passed the order up to the finance department for the payment process.

When the finance department came to buy the Swiss francs

forward they discovered that it was at a premium against sterling of 6.95 per cent, whereas if the buyer had bought in France the French franc was at a discount against sterling of 10.51 per cent. While there was virtually no difference in the cost of buying the two products, there was a difference of 17.46 per cent in the cost of buying the two currencies.

As in the case of exports this is but one example highlighting the appalling lack of training provided to buyers in most of our companies. No blame whatsoever can be attached to them for no one seems to have thought it necessary to train them in this field.

Figure 42 is a very good example of the situation that arose in the early 1980s. The world was in the doldrums including the most powerful economy in the West. The new administration in the USA recognised the need for them to take the initiative and act as the locomotive to pull the Western world out of the recession. This would take a great deal of money, however, and they therefore set out to attract as much of the world's surplus liquid funds as possible. They achieved this by lifting the prime rate of interest to an almost record high thereby making the reward for investing in dollars very substantial.

This policy had the desired effect. As the demand for dollars grew the exchange rate began to come down and eventually came very close to parity with sterling, i.e. $1 = £1.

While the spot rate of the dollar was coming down, however, the forward rate was at a substantial discount against sterling simply because the dollar interest rate (domestic as well as Euro) was considerably higher than sterling interest rates.

Figure 42 illustrates the advantage which a British buyer had at that time when buying from Japan. If he negotiated the purchase in yen and bought the yen forward he would have paid a premium of 4.018 per cent, whereas if he had negotiated the purchase in US dollars, and the Japanese were happy to accept dollars, he would have bought the dollars forward at a discount of 5.31 per cent thus providing a total saving of 9.328 per cent.

Figure 43 shows that although the dollar interest rates had come down considerably, they were still higher than sterling interest rates in 1983 and as a result the dollar was at a discount.

Figure 42

---

14 August 1981: £100,000 purchase from Japan
Yen spot 456.90 = £1 ∴ yen 45,690,000
1 year 439.00   = £1   cost £104,018
US $ spot 2.0865= £1 ∴ US $ 208,650
1 year 2.2035   = £1   cost £94,690

Saving in cost £9,328 = 9.328%

Figure 43

Import from Taiwan, November 1983
Quoted: £0.49 or US$0.73
@ Forward rate $1.509 = £1
US$0.73 = £0.484

Saving in year £50,000

This is a case of a British company importing small unit components from Taiwan and placing firm scheduled annual contracts. The supplier had always sold in sterling at a very competitive price. In November 1983, when the buyer was negotiating a new annual contract he asked his Taiwanese supplier to quote him a US dollar price as well as a sterling price. This he did by converting the sterling price into dollars at the spot rate and providing prices of 49 pence and 73 cents per unit. The buyer then bought the dollars at a forward rate of $1.5090 = £1 producing a price of 48.4 pence per unit and saved himself approximately £50,000 on his annual contract.

This case is almost the perfect example of what this technology is all about. Big additional profit margins of 21 per cent on sales are impressive and underline the urgent need for our sales and purchasing executives to understand the technology and how to apply it to their commercial transactions, but this particular case is almost the perfect illustration of its everyday uses.

Figure 44 tells the story of a subsidiary of a large group of companies with a highly sophisticated treasury department at its head office which is extremely well versed in all aspects of managing the group's currency exposure.

Figure 44

Import order

Buying forward DM£2,277,379
FF£2,185,833
Reductions against DM – 4.04%

The subsidiary, however, was far from sophisticated in its understanding of foreign exchange and while importing all its basic raw material from France, the buyer had been paying the French supplier for many years in Deutschmarks. When asked why in Deutschmarks and not in French francs he had to admit he did not know but did it really make any difference?

The company exported a high proportion of its output but as profit margins in the trade were very small, approximately 4 per cent, and owing to the very keen competition there was a fairly constant cry from the salesmen of 'can we shave the price?'

On having the French supplier's confirmation that he would happily accept payment in French francs, the buyer found that by paying in French francs instead of Deutschmarks and buying them forward he could achieve a reduction in his cost of purchase of 4.04 per cent; as big a margin as the profit margin on the sale of the finished product.

The significance of this is best judged with reference to Figure 45 showing that a reduction in the cost of purchases of as little as 2 per cent can make as big a difference as 10 per cent more profit on the sale of the finished product.

Moreover, this group is no different from many others whose highly sophisticated treasury departments rarely have the time,

Figure 45

$$\text{Cost} - 2\% = \text{Profit} + 10\%$$

---

the resources in manpower nor the practical experience to train the personnel in their subsidiaries. Some try to overcome this problem by inviting their bank to send someone from the foreign exchange department to talk to them. While such a speaker will obviously have a great deal of knowledge about the activities of foreign exchange dealers, his audience is not particularly mindful of becoming foreign exchange dealers but merely seek to understand how they can apply what goes on inside a foreign exchange dealing room to their kind of commercial transaction. Unfortunately, however, this is an area in which such a speaker will rarely have much experience. This, alas, is the yawning gap which has now persisted for many years and if this book can begin the process of bridging that gap then indeed it will have succeeded.

Figures 46 and 47 tell the sad story of a company which did not protect itself against the exchange risk on its imports. It placed orders worth £10m each in April 1986 with German and Japanese suppliers but payable in Deutschmarks and yen. If they had bought the currencies forward they would have paid premiums of approximately £300,000 for each currency. When they came to buy the currencies in September, however, they paid an extra £1,924,398 for the Deutschmarks and an extra £1,756,756 for the yen.

Figure 46

DM imports, April–September 1986

Spot DM3.47 = £1 – 2.91 = £1
£10m order placed for DM34,700,000

Cost £11,924,398
6 months forward premium £300,000

Figure 47

Yen imports, April–September 1986

Spot yen 261 = £1 – 222 = £1
£10m order placed for yen 2610m

Cost £11,756,756
6 months forward premium £300,000

Some might argue that while you lose some, you win some and if the exchange rates had gone the other way they would have been applauded. Not so. An exchange risk is *not* a commercial risk, there is no way of assessing it.

The situation was well summarised by the chief foreign exchange dealer of a leading London bank when confronted by the chairman of a large engineering group who was in the habit of taking a view on what exchange rates were likely to do in the future, 'Well, I make the rates, but I don't guess what they are going to be next week. What do you base your guess on?'

At an annual general meeting, a bad guess may be given the aura of respectability by such words as 'due to adverse currency movement', whereas 'we gambled and lost' might be nearer the mark. Conversely, when a company has protected itself by using the forward market but the rate went in its favour thus producing a situation where it would have made more money if it had not protected itself, again this may be reported as a loss due to adverse currency movements whereas it might be more accurately reported as, 'if we had gambled we would have made more money'.

21　The Treasury Function

There are two kinds of exposure to exchange risks which need to be managed:

(a)　The translation exposure, i.e. translating the value of overseas assets from one currency into another.
(b)　The transaction exposure, i.e. the exchange risks arising from sales and/or purchases.

The main object of this book is to help exporters and importers to understand foreign exchange sufficiently to be able to obtain maximum benefit from using the available facilities. It can only therefore impinge on the treasury function in respect of the transaction exposure and the relationship between 'finance', 'sales' and 'purchasing'.

There is an increasing tendency in larger companies to establish a central or group treasury department which will act as a bank for all UK based subsidiaries and/or divisions. Provided that such a department is buying unto itself the group's transaction exchange risks by buying and selling forward at the current spot and forward rates as opposed to fictitious internal rates this can only be of great assistance to the trading subsidiaries and divisions. By so doing, the group treasury department can go into the money market and trade in much larger sums than each division could do on its own and consequently provide the keenest rates. Moreover, it will have continuing up-to-date information on all currency transactions.

In many such treasury departments, however, there seems to be some reluctance in providing the subsidiaries and/or divisions with Euro-currency borrowing facilities whereas they can freely use the forward market. In many cases there are substantial administrative advantages in using a currency overdraft as opposed to the forward market and it should be perfectly feasible for the treasury to provide this. Moreover, in many such groups, borrowing facilities are provided by the treasury department to the trading units at no cost although each is considered its own profit centre. In such circumstances therefore there is little incentive for the trading units to reduce their cost of borrowing and they are therefore reluctant to sell in foreign currencies. Consequently the group as a whole is losing very substantial advantages.

Problems can arise where the treasury adopts a purely advisory role and advises the subsidiaries and/or divisions as to whether they should cover their exchange risk or not as the case may be in relation to what the treasury thinks the rate is likely to do. Trading divisions should not be expected to take any exchange risk. It is up to the treasury to manage the exposure and having bought the group's exchange risk the treasury becomes its own profit centre and should manage the total exposure as it sees fit using all the techniques available to it and with responsibility to the board of directors.

One of the main features of a successful treasury department is to establish good communications and working relationships between itself and sales and purchasing departments. This can provide up-to-date briefings for executives who are about to embark on overseas negotiations and a corresponding inflow of relevant market and buyer information which can be vital to the credit controller.

No company would normally approach any of its suppliers without having a very good idea as to what it requires from them and the competitive price. Banks are also suppliers and yet many companies sometimes approach them, particularly on matters of foreign exchange, with little or no idea of what they require let alone the cost. As a result it has been known for mistakes and misunderstandings to arise. In order to avoid this it is up to the treasury department to ensure that when contacting the bank with regard to a forward transaction for example, it should have done the sums and have a good idea of what the premium or discount should be.

22 Strategic Considerations

Exports

Assuming that the policy decision to sell in foreign currencies has been made, the first consideration must be based on the type of product or industry with which the company is involved. The considerations are obviously different between say a manufacturer of small unit consumer goods and a company only involved in major construction projects. The type of buyer to whom you are selling should therefore give rise to the first consideration.

Figure 48

Strategic considerations – exports

Selling to (a) own company (b) distributor
(c) end user

(a) Sell in buyer's currency – ensure you make any premium – consider ECU.

(b) Essential to sell in his currency – if not he is bound to load local currency price and your product will be uncompetitive

(c) Sell in his currency or any major currency to which his may be more closely allied

---

Selling to your own subsidiary

There seems to be a very mixed view among companies which have established their own companies overseas. One view taken is that because they are wholly owned it is therefore better to sell to them in sterling, even if sales to third party buyers are conducted in currency, and leave them to decide whether to cover the risk or not. Another view seems to be that because they are wholly owned one should sell to them in their own currency while continuing to sell to third party buyers in sterling. In some cases it is even assumed that if neither party takes any action the exchange risk becomes self-insuring and disappears!

In the case of the former, there is no difference between an overseas buyer which is owned and one which is not owned. In both cases they are having to reconcile their local positions to local currency so why give them the exchange risk? The local facilities for dealing with the risk will certainly be nothing like as good as those available in London if they exist at all. In any event, local management may not be sufficiently well versed in the technology to know how to deal with the risk and may simply rely on loading the local currency price as their means of protection thereby making them less competitive or less profitable than they need be.

Alternatively local management may be tempted to run the exchange risk and only go into the forward market if and when they feel the exchange rate is likely to go against them. If the subsidiary is located in the USA its management may prefer to use the financial futures or currency option market which are considerably more expensive than the forward market.

A parent company which is domiciled in Britain has the best facilities available and should therefore retain control of the situation. It can thereby ensure that maximum benefit is achieved by way of forward premiums or borrowings in currency, which benefits can easily be passed on to the subsidiary if required. If the parent passes on the exchange risk it could be tempting the subsidiaries to speculate at the parent's expense.

With the approach of 1992, any company with a distribution network throughout Europe consisting either of wholly-owned subsidiaries or independents will need to consider establishing European prices denominated in ECUs. This will be particularly important if those subsidiaries and/or independents are themselves selling across frontiers.

Selling to distributors

As already indicated, it is essential to sell to any buyer overseas who is distributing the product, in his own currency. If he is expected to carry the exchange risk, he will invariably protect himself simply by loading the local currency price and thereby reduce the product's competitiveness and market penetration. Experience has shown that in countries whose currencies tend to be rather volatile, it is even more important to sell in local currencies as otherwise local distributors, and even subsidiaries, will sometimes feel it necessary to load the local currency price by as much as 20 per cent. These countries do not, of course, include those in South and Central America, for example, where special considerations prevail.

There is a forward market in London for most convertible currencies and even if they are at a discount, which may have to be added to the currency price, this discount will rarely be anything like as great as the loading which the distributor is likely to add.

When selling to distributors in developing countries or in those whose currencies are not readily convertible, the US dollar may be the best choice. Bearing in mind that IMF and World Bank loans are denominated in US dollars it is preferable to sell to these countries in dollars rather than sterling. While the oil business is closely geared to the US dollar, the currencies of the major oil producing countries may also be used and there is normally a forward market for most of them in London.

Selling to end-users

The main consideration here should be, 'what currency to which country?'

Sales to the major economies should normally be transacted in the buyer's own currency. Exporters into Europe, however, should be mindful of the ECU. There is already a growing volume of business being transacted in ECUs.

In the pre-glasnost era buying agencies in the Comecon countries tended to pool their resources of hard currencies and then to buy in the currency of which they held a surplus. Moreover, they

Figure 49

Strategic considerations – exports

What currency to which country?

Major developed economies	Their own
Major oil producers	Their own
Inter-European sales	ECUs
Countries receiving IMF World bank loans	US dollar
Other developing countries	US dollar
Comecon countries	All major currencies
Ex-colonial countries	Colonist currency

---

usually tended to assume that exporters expected to be paid in their own currency. A UK exporter traditionally selling in sterling therefore was at a disadvantage if the buying agency happened to be buying at that time in say Deutschmarks or dollars. In the light of current developments it is very important for UK exporters to make sure that buyers in Eastern Bloc countries know and understand that they are prepared to accept payment in any of the major currencies.

In some countries initial research is required to ascertain which currency would be the buyer's first choice. In Turkey, for example, there is a considerable volume of Deutschmarks being repatriated by a large work-force of Turks in Germany. It may well be easier for the Turkish buyer to buy Deutschmarks rather than sterling.

Similarly, in some large contracts, it is possible to have a contractor of one country employed by an agency of another country and the contractor employing a sub-contractor from a third country who may in turn be buying from a supplier in a fourth country. In these circumstances where the exporter may have four currencies to choose from it is essential before even quoting for him to know in which currency he should deal or which currency will produce the keenest price for him.

Where does the competition come from?

Figure 50

Strategic considerations – exports

Where does the competition come from?
If from premium currency countries
calculate forward rates before
going to negotiate

This is a key question to which any exporter should have the answer before he quotes and/or starts to negotiate. Bearing in mind that a premium is merely a reflection of the fact that the other country's interest rate is lower than sterling and also bearing in mind that we have had, and continue to have, the highest interest rate than any other of the major economies, he may well be able to meet the competition by switching into the competitor's currency, selling it forward and giving away part, if not all, of the premium involved. (Refer to Case Studies, p.00)

No sales executive should venture abroad in order to negotiate and try to win an overseas contract without knowing from which countries the competition comes and without having calculated the kind of premium that would accrue on the forward rate of the currency or currencies if there is more than one competitor. If the overseas buyer is thinking of buying from say Germany or Japan, he will have to pay them in Deutschmarks or yen. He can therefore equally pay the UK exporter in Deutschmarks or yen. The UK exporter, however, has the advantage in so far that he can sell their currencies forward at a premium.

Are the other currencies at a premium or discount?

You will have seen how essential it may be for the executive to know before he sets out on his mission whether the buyer's currency, or that of any competitor, is at a premium or discount. It is equally essential for him to know how that premium or discount has been moving so that he can project it reasonably safely over the period during which he will be negotiating. If he is going to be away for say a month, the spot rate of exchange may well move during this period. The really valuable information for him to know, however, is that whatever the spot rate does during that month, the premium or discount has gone with it, i.e. the interest rates have not moved significantly.

Monitoring the interest rates, as shown in Figure 12 (p.00) is an invaluable guide and shows that whereas the premium on the Deutschmark against sterling in October 1988 was 7 per cent per annum, by July 1989 it was still about 7 per cent per annum. Briefing himself with these figures, the exporter would be able to say to himself that whatever the spot rate may do over the next month, I am going to have a premium of at least say 6 per cent per annum. The premium will therefore fulfil two functions. It will act as a built-in cushion in the event of the Deutschmark being devalued against sterling during his negotiations or it may be used to reduce the price.

Imports

The best supplier technically

It is thought to have been said a long time ago that the British were a nation of eccentrics. If it was possible for them to do anything the hard way, or even the wrong way, they did not usually fail! This seems to be echoed to some extent in our exporting and importing practices. In order to obtain maximum benefit from the technology of foreign exchange, for whose invention and development we can largely lay claim, we should be exporting wherever possible in foreign currencies and paying for our imports in sterling. Instead of which we still mainly export in sterling and pay for our imports almost entirely in foreign currencies. This means in the main we continue to lose the benefit of the premiums arising from the lower interest rates in other countries and pay the premiums due to the higher interest rates in this country.

This disparity is even more noticeable among importers than exporters and it therefore seems even more essential for buyers to become expert in the use of this technology. It does not do for them merely to pass the buck to 'finance', nor to assume that our overseas suppliers would refuse to supply us if we insisted on paying in sterling.

The first consideration however must be, 'who is the best supplier from a technical standpoint?' But there are other important considerations which may have a vital impact on cost.

Alternative suppliers and their currencies

If the buyer is in the habit of always buying from the same supplier and has been successful in establishing a good relationship over a long period, he should nevertheless be careful to keep note of suppliers in other countries and in particular the cost of buying forward the currencies concerned. If he is casting around for a new supplier one of the important considerations which he should also take into account is the cost of buying the currency. He should continually be aware of opportunities appearing in other countries not only by virtue of movements in his favour of exchange rates, but also by virtue of lower premiums and even more so discounts. For example, in 1982 while the Japanese yen was at a premium of 5.06 per cent per annum the Deutschmark was only at a premium of 3.56 but the Italian lira and French franc were at discounts of 10.39 and 6.91 per cent per annum respectively.

If the purchase could have been made from Germany instead of Japan or better still from Italy or France, the cost could have been reduced very considerably.

In September 1989, the yen was at a premium of 7.82 per cent per annum while the Deutschmark was at a premium of 6.27 per cent, the lira at a premium of 1.64 per cent and the peseta at a discount of 0.71 per cent per annum.

Many senior engineers, however, are quite unaware of these potential advantages and merely instruct the buyer to place an order for 'that' product with 'that' supplier and woebetide any buyer who thinks differently. This is unfortunate and should be discouraged particularly if the buyer has taken the trouble to do his research properly.

Figure 51 shows quotes in US dollars, Deutschmarks and pesetas converted into sterling at the forward rates and compared with a UK sterling price of £10,000. This will immediately indicate to the buyer that the Spanish peseta price shows a saving in cost of 1.75 per cent over the German and 1.36 per cent over the American.

Figure 51

Strategic considerations – imports

Alternative supplier countries/currencies
Local UK price £10,000

Sterling price in $ £10,122 (+1.22%)
DM £10,161 (+1.61%) Peseta £9,986 (−0.14%)

Purchasing tactics

Having established the best supplier in terms of quality, price and delivery, the buyer should obtain a quote in the supplier's own currency where that currency is freely convertible and for which there is a forward market. If it is a country whose currency is not readily acceptable then he should obtain a quote in say US dollars or sterling. If it is an ex-colony, its currency may still be linked to the old colonial power.

It is important for the buyer to know the currency price of the product so that he can negotiate from strength. Knowing the currency price and if the currency is at a premium, he might then ask the supplier to quote him a sterling price to see whether this has been converted at the spot rate of exchange, the forward rate or a heavily loaded rate. Figures 52 and 53 show the three alternatives. If the Deutschmark quote of DM30,700 has been converted at (A), the spot rate, the buyer has got a good deal, if at (B), the three months forward rate, he will at least know that the supplier knows about the forward market and he might then negotiate to pay only half the premium so that they share the cost of the currency equally between them. He should certainly not pay more. If the supplier refuses to quote him any kind of sterling price, this will be a confirmation that he does not understand the forward market.

If the supplier quotes a sterling price converted at a heavily loaded rate (C), this will tell him again that his supplier knows nothing of the forward market and that he is merely concerned

Figure 52

Strategic considerations – imports

Obtain quote in supplier's currency
DM30,700

Request quote in sterling
(A) £10,000
(B) £10,161
(C) £10,500

Figure 53

Strategic considerations – imports

If deciding on Germany, in the case of

(a) Accept
(b) Negotiate at £10,080
(c) Make final offer £10,100

---

with having a cushion in the price in order to cover the exchange risk. It is now therefore a matter of negotiating the size of the cushion and the buyer can do this by making a sterling offer converted at a rate much closer to the spot rate than the supplier's loaded rate and closer than the forward rate. This is a negotiating ploy which has already been used successfully and is particularly relevant if used when the buyer is about to place a firm order.

If the supplier has quoted a sterling price in the first place, the buyer is immediately at a disadvantage. If he does not know the currency price he will not be able to calculate the rate at which the currency price was converted into sterling. He should therefore make every endeavour to find out the local currency price from say other suppliers in that country.

If the supplier's currency can be bought forward at a discount this will have the effect of reducing the landed cost of the product and it is this cost calculated at the forward rate that reflects the true cost. If the buyer is not immediately about to place an order but will be doing so in the future, then as in the case of the exporter, he should monitor the Euro-currency interest rates as shown in Figure 12 (p.00) so that he can make a reasonably accurate projection of what the discount is likely to be when he comes to place a firm order.

23   Buying from UK Importing Agents

If the UK exporters sell to their distributing agents overseas in sterling, the distributors will invariably protect themselves against the exchange risk by loading the local currency price. UK distributing agents for overseas suppliers will very often do exactly the same, as in company with many other British exporters and importers, they do not understand the forward market. As a result, the loading can sometimes be as high as 15 or 20 per cent but in any event it is much more likely to be more than the amount of any premium involved in the forward purchase of the currency.

The amount of the loading will depend on the stability of the currency involved. If the importer is buying from those countries whose currencies tend to be volatile he will tend to increase the loading because the risk of the exchange rates moving against him is considerably higher. If on the other hand, he is importing from countries with very stable currencies the loading may be minimal.

Irrespective of where the goods originate, the ultimate UK buyer of those goods should understand the technology of foreign exchange sufficiently well to know what the forward rate is and thereby ensure that he is not paying more than he need. There is no reason why he should not even enquire from the importing agent whether he is buying the currency forward or not. Figure 54 illustrates a case where the importing agent was buying from Italy and whereas he could have bought the lire forward at a discount he was loading the sterling price by as much as 20 per cent.

Figure 54

Strategic considerations – imports

Imported goods bought from local agents

Italian product sold at £12,000
Agent added 20% for Forex risk
He could have bought forward
for £9,792

You must know the currency price
before you buy

---

24 Conclusion

We have in the past allowed far too many of our sales and purchasing executives to travel overseas conducting business across national frontiers with little or virtually no knowledge of how the foreign exchange aspect will affect their transactions.

The evidence suggests that this technology should no longer be the exclusive prerogative of the finance department/treasury. It constitutes an essential part of any company's overseas marketing, pricing and purchasing strategy. It has a direct bearing on the way in which overseas sales and purchases are transacted. It seems essential therefore that all those executives concerned should be sufficiently well trained in its application so as to be able to conduct their negotiations with the utmost skill and conviction thereby placing themselves at all times in the strongest possible negotiating position especially when having to combat stiff competition.

There can be little doubt that anyone involved in overseas sales or purchases who is not fully versed in this technology is at a considerable disadvantage and cannot therefore be expected to achieve the very best results for his company. There is unfortunately still a fairly wide held view however, that such personnel cannot really be fully trusted with such complex matters as foreign exchange. 'Let them just sell the product without giving them all this extra to think about', is a too common reaction by senior management.

In this age of high technology such views can no longer be justified and can only lead to the kind of wasted opportunity illustrated in this book. Besides, experience has proved that once they have mastered the technology, such salesmen and buyers rapidly grow in confidence and stature and soon reap the rewards of negotiating from strength. The realisation that he knows more about foreign exchange than his opposite number acts as a spur to strike the best possible deal, and the knowledge that he has succeeded in striking the best possible deal gives him the best possible satisfaction. He is a much too valuable member of any company team to be denied that reward.

Glossary

American option   A currency option which can be exercised at any time up to the expiry date.

Arbitrage   Dealing between two trading centres in order to make a profit arising from a difference in rates at the two centres.

At the Money   A currency option with a strike price equal to the current exchange rate.

Bid   Normally the rate at which the market maker is willing to buy a currency.

Bretton Woods   The location in the USA where a conference was held in 1944 to establish the International Monetary Fund and provide the means for the future economic reconstruction of the wartorn areas of the world.

Broker   Introduces business from one bank to another, either buyers and sellers or borrowers and lenders. He is paid a commission for so doing by both parties.

Call option   The right but not the obligation to buy the currency which is the subject of the option.

Certificates of deposit (CDs)   A certificate issued by a bank with which a deposit has been made. It gives title of the deposited funds together with interest to the holder and can be traded accordingly.

Commission   Charge made by a bank to execute a foreign

exchange contract. When Britain still had exchange controls commissions were regulated at one per mille on the value of the transaction with a maximum of £10 any one transaction. Since the lifting of exchange controls, commissions are a matter of negotiation between the bank and its clients in the same way as general bank charges.

Confirmation   After transacting a foreign exchange deal over the telephone or telex, the parties to the deal send to each other written confirmation giving full details of the transaction.

Convertible currency   Currency which can be freely exchanged for other currencies without special authorisation from the appropriate central bank.

Cross rate   Exchange rate between two foreign currencies. For example, when a dealer in London buys or sells Deutschmarks against US dollars as opposed to sterling.

Discount   When the interest rate of the home-based currency is lower than that of the foreign currency involved in a forward transaction.

Drawdown   Used in relation to a loan – term or overdraft denotes the actual payment to the borrower which may be at a later stage than when the loan was originally agreed.

ECGD   Export Credit Guarantee Department. A government agency, which may be privatised, which insures exporters against loss arising from commercial and political risks.

Euro-currency   Currency held outside its own country.

European option   An option which can only be exercised on the expiry date.

Exchange contract   Verbal or written agreement between two parties to deliver one currency in exchange for another.

Expiry date   The final date on which a currency option can be exercised.

Firm quotation   When a bank gives a firm selling and/or buying rate for immediate acceptance or with a time limit.

Floating exchange rate   When the value of a currency is decided by market forces.

Forward contract   Agreement between two parties to deliver one currency in exchange for another either on a future date or between two future dates.

Forward limit   Normally a cumulative limit up to which a bank will agree to transact forward sales and/or purchases.

Hedge   Action taken to reduce or eliminate a currency exposure.

Indication   When a bank gives a spot or forward rate of exchange for information only and does not intend it as a quotation. Similarly, if the client wants a rate purely for information purposes he should ask for an 'indication' only.

In the money   In a currency option when the strike price is better than the current exchange rate.

Intervention   When a central bank goes into the market to buy or sell a currency in order to influence the exchange rate.

Libor   London Interbank Offered Rate. The rate at which principal London banks offer to lend currency to one another. Often used as the basis for fixing the interest on bank loans.

LIFFE The London International Financial Futures Exchange.

Mandate Before a company can begin trading in the forward market, its bank will normally require a formal authority from the company stipulating *inter alia* the name(s) of the person(s) who are authorised to commit the company and the amounts up to which they are authorised to do so.

Maturity date Date when settlement between the two contracting parties is due.

Option (a) In a forward contract when it is agreed that the currency will be delivered or taken up between two fixed dates in the future. (b) An instrument whereby the buyer of the option has the right but not the obligation to buy or sell currency at a fixed rate of exchange for an agreed period, or borrow currency at an agreed interest rate.

At par Where the Euro-currency interest rates are the same and hence there is no premium of discount on the forward sale or purchase of the currency and the forward rate is the same as the spot rate.

Point (a) One hundredth part of one cent. For example, if the exchange rate moves from US $1.5822 to US $1.5825 it is often referred to as a move of three points. (b) It also denotes the movement of 1 per cent in interest rates, i.e. from 10 per cent to 11 per cent per annum.

Premium (a) When the interest rate of the home-based currency is higher than that of the foreign currency involved in a forward transaction. (b) The fee involved in the purchase of a currency option.

Put option The right but not the obligation to sell the currency which is the subject of the option.

Rollover   Sometimes used to mean 'extending' a forward contract but usually used when extending the maturity of a loan.

Special Drawing Rights (SDRs).   Conceived in the late 1960s by the IMF as a means of offsetting imbalances between central banks. SDRs had a fixed gold value equivalent at the time to one US dollar.

Settlement risk   The event of an exporter or importer failing to meet his obligation under a forward contract resulting in a loss at the time of settlement. It is this risk against which the bank covers itself by imposing a cumulative limit on the client's forward deals.

Smithsonian Agreement   Derives its name from the Smithsonian Institute building in Washington where an agreement was reached in 1971 by the world's ten leading industrialised countries to meet a proposed devaluation of the US dollar against gold and for many of the major currencies to return to fixed rates of exchange in line with the new devalued dollar.

Swap   A transaction involving the simultaneous buying and selling of a currency for different maturity dates such as when a forward transaction is being extended.

Town cheque.   A sterling cheque drawn on the City branch of a London clearing bank. For sums of £100,000 or over, it is possible for these to be cleared for value on the same day. For sums below £100,000 together with Country cheques, any sterling cheque drawn on a UK bank other than a Town cheque, the normal period for these to be cleared for value is three clear working days.

Transaction exposure   The exposure to exchange risk arising from a commercial transaction, i.e. the buying or selling of goods or services.

Translation exposure   The exposure to exchange risk arising from the translation of the value of an asset from one currency to another.

Value   Date on which a transaction has value. For example, the drawing of a cheque does not give 'value' to the amount involved until the cheque has been cleared.

Quick Reference Index